REFLECTIONS

REFLECTIONS

Auschwitz, Memory, and a Life Recreated

Agi Rubin

Henry Greenspan

First Edition 2006

Published in the United States by
Paragon House
1925 Oakcrest Avenue, Suite 7
St. Paul, MN 55113

Cover print "By a Thread II" by Lynne Avadenka, © Lynne Avadenka, used
courtesy of Lynne Avadenka. Photo by R.H. Hensleigh.

Library of Congress Cataloging-in-Publication Data

    Rubin, Agi, 1929-
      Reflections : Auschwitz, memory, and a life recreated / Agi Rubin,
    Henry Greenspan. -- 1st ed. 2006.
      p. cm.
    ISBN 1-55778-861-8 (pbk. : alk. paper) 1. Rubin, Agi, 1929- 2.
    Jews--Ukraine--Mukacheve--Biography. 3. Holocaust, Jewish (1939-
    1945)--Ukraine--Mukacheve--Personal narratives. 4. Holocaust
    survivors--United States--Biography. I. Greenspan, Henry, 1948- II.
    Title.
    DS135.U43R835 2006
    940.53'18092--dc22
    [B]
                         2006013078

Manufactured in the United States of America
10 9 8 7 6 5 4 3 2 1

The paper used in this publication meets the minimum requirements of American National Standard for Information Sciences—Permanence of Paper for
Printed Library Materials, ANSIZ39.48-1984.

For current information about all releases from Paragon House,
visit the web site at http://www.paragonhouse.com

As an account of atrocities, therefore, this book adds nothing to what is already known.... [I]t should be able, rather, to furnish documentation for a quiet study of certain aspects of the human mind.

PRIMO LEVI
Survival in Auschwitz

This book is dedicated to the memory of all my loved ones who perished in the Holocaust.

The writing that became these pages began right after Liberation, in 1945. Now, sixty years later, the work has been completed. I leave it for my children—Vicki, Amy, Randy—and for my grandchildren: Rivky, Shmuel, Moshe, Devora, Miriam, Justin, and Jeremy.

Thanks to Henry Greenspan for his friendship and his long collaboration in this project. We brought it to light together.

Most of all, thanks to my husband, Zoli, for his love and encouragement over all these years.

AGI RUBIN

To special friends—John Roth, Sid Bolkosky, Lori Bolkosky, Rob Cohen, Darone Ruskay, Andy Greenspan, Michael Berenbaum, Lynne Avadenka, and Nancy Rosenfeld.

For Nancy, in all ways.

In Carol's memory.

For Agi, my teacher and friend.

HENRY GREENSPAN

Contents

REUNIONS

APPENDICES

Foreword

You are about to read one of the most remarkable books to emerge from the Holocaust, Nazi Germany's genocidal attempt to destroy the Jewish people. *Reflections: Auschwitz, Memory, and a Life Recreated* is the result of a one-of-a-kind interaction between Agi Rubin, an eloquent survivor of that catastrophe, and Henry Greenspan, a Holocaust scholar whose in-depth probing of survivor testimony has been pioneering and penetrating in ways that are unsurpassed.

Ethical insight as well as historical knowledge about the Holocaust depend on access to archives, those repositories of information and evidence that document what happened. Rubin and Greenspan show that no archive is more fundamental than human memory itself. That judgment does not mean that human memory is infallible; nor is memory a substitute for the records that historians examine when they do their essential archival research about the Holocaust. Nevertheless, absent human memory and the critical reflection that emerges from it, archival records would be mute and meaningless. In that sense, archives would be closed even if their vaults and files were open.

Reflections takes its reader into a memory-archive that is as deep as it is open, as revealing as it is layered, as complex as it is brief and simple, as disconcerting and challenging as it is intense and poignant. Minimalist in their use of words spare and lean, Rubin and Greenspan together have crafted a Holocaust document whose impact includes the absences and silences that their voices evoke. Not only are these pages open in ways that reveal the vulnerability of their authors but also the episodes and vignettes, the images and scenes, open us to honest encounters with persons and places that can move us profoundly.

Rubin and Greenspan chose words from Primo Levi, another eloquent survivor of Auschwitz, to serve as their book's governing epigraph. Speaking of *Survival in Auschwitz*, his masterful memoir about the Holocaust, Levi suggested that his book furnished "documentation for a quiet study of certain aspects of the human mind" rather than an account of previously unknown atrocities. Like Levi's writing, *Reflections* is also a deeply psychological work whose revelations emerged fully through a long life after the Holocaust. Those insights beckon us to reflect deeply on our own lives, warning us to take nothing good for granted as we do.

—John K. Roth
Edward J. Sexton Professor of Philosophy
Director, The Center for the Study of the Holocaust,
Genocide, and Human Rights
Claremont McKenna College

Introduction

Reflections is a book of memories, but it is equally a book *about* memory, both during the Holocaust and after. In the midst of the destruction, the task was to remember some fragment of care and safety that one had known before. For many, such memories could be recaptured in dreams, and only partially even there. Thus Agi Rubin describes a recurring dream she had in Auschwitz:

> It always came and went the same way. I was sitting in my mother's lap. She was there. And I was trying, once more, to burrow into her corner of protection. But, at the same moment, the fence of Auschwitz was also there, the barbed wire. And that's how the dream always ended—with the image of the fence. The good, sheltered feeling was fragile. Even in a dream, its boundaries were invaded every time. It was as much as I could salvage.

Fragile and compromised as it was, that much Agi *did* salvage. The dream reformed, dissolved, reformed, dissolved—a corner of protection alternately lost and found throughout the Auschwitz night.

Inside Auschwitz, Agi struggled to remember shelter and belonging. After Auschwitz, the role of memory was more complicated. On one side, being able to recapture experiences from before the destruction remained critical. For many survivors, simply recalling having once been cherished was the foundation upon which they rebuilt their lives. Even that much, however, could not always be retrieved and, once retrieved, was not easy to sustain. The Holocaust not only lived on in memory but, often enough, threatened to overwhelm all the rest. Agi notes:

> We survivors are bundles of contradictions…We push away the past, and we are constantly drawn back to it. When we are here, we are also there. And when we are there, we are also here…And even the past is split in two—memories of home, which we usually try to recapture; and memories of the destruction of home, which we usually try to forget.

> So there are many strands at once. One world reminds us of the other; one thought leads to the next, and into the past….It is not that our joys are not real. They are entirely real. It is just that they never exist simply by themselves. They are always in reference to something else, something that can consume them in an instant.

Survivors, Agi tells us, are jugglers. In some unsteady balance, life goes on, death goes on, and survivors go on—somewhere in between.

What is it like to live within such contradictions? How does one manage them over the course of an entire life? Notwithstanding all that has been written by and about Holocaust survivors, we have rarely heard. Most survivor memoirs end at liberation or include only a brief coda about what followed. In *Reflections*, the emphasis is reversed. Agi describes in detail her initial awakening and the journey home, being a young survivor in the giddy limbo of postwar Europe, recreating lives and families in the United States, responding to the unanticipated surge of interest in the Holocaust in recent years. Throughout, Agi's conversation with memories—both those that sustain and those that undo—deepens. "New experiences reflect old ones," she notes. "They put them in a different light, or a different darkness."

What is perhaps most remarkable about Agi's reflections is that they began in the first hours of liberation. In April 1945, barely forty-eight hours after surviving one of the death marches that followed the evacuation of Auschwitz, Agi began a diary. She was then sixteen years old and wrote about the terror she had just endured. Almost unique within survivors' writing, this record was inscribed at the very moment of beginning to awaken from the nightmare.

At that time, and more fully as the years went on, Agi would discover the awakening would never be complete. In one passage from the liberation diary she writes: "Up until the last moment, the crematorium is our nightmare. We are telling everybody about it, whether we want to or not. Either in my dreams or when I am awake, I see only the flames in front of me. And the vision never fades." And yet, bundle of contradictions, the very next day, Agi writes: "We talk about the past and the future. And the future and the past. We have suffered enough. Now good will come. Let the sunshine brighten our life." Already, Holocaust memory and Agi's new life were beginning to separate. Distant as they became in time, however, Agi would learn that they would never be apart.

That interweaving of past and present is retold in *Reflections*. Although Agi did not keep a diary regularly, she returned to her journal periodically over the years, often on the anniversary of the liberation—one year later, five years later, twenty years later. Her liberation diary as well as these later pages are all included in what follows. So, also, are Agi's still later reflections as she reread her journals—that is, her thoughts as she looked back at herself, looking back. All of these circles of reflection are central to the story this book tells about Auschwitz, memory, and a life recreated.

Reflections, then, emerges from a continuing conversation between memory and an unfolding present. It also emerges from a continuing conversation between two friends, our own conversations over twenty-five years. In significant ways, the two dialogues are intertwined. "Memory is born in conversation," Agi notes. "For remembering, I need your questions, the spark of conversation, fully to bring it out. Then memories take their shape and find their words. They emerge between us."

I turn, then, to some of my own reflections on our friendship and our collaboration. This book has two authors because page by page, even word by word, we did, indeed, write it together. The life retold in *Reflections* is entirely Agi's. So also are its insights, its convictions, and its wisdom. But the retelling itself came to life, as Agi said, "between us."

I first met Agi in 1979, and I remember the evening well. I was at a program about survivors' experiences soon after liberation, and the speakers included Agi, another survivor, and a social worker who had been active in Jewish relief efforts immediately after the war. The social worker was obviously well meaning, but her talk betrayed a condescension toward survivors that was almost universal in the early years. Referring to the survivors (almost as though the two sitting next to her were not there), she recalled, "To be honest, we really didn't know how to handle them. We didn't know how to handle the survivors at that time." I can still hear Agi's response. "We didn't realize," she noted pointedly, "that we had to be 'handled.'" Here was someone whom I knew I wanted to get to know.

Agi and I met a few weeks later. I had been interviewing survivors as part of my dissertation research, and she had agreed to talk with me. It was during our second interview, as I recall, that she first showed me—actually read to me, translating from Hungarian as she went—some of what she had written during the first hours of liberation. I was stunned. First, because such a record existed. Second, because Agi's reflections have a natural poetry and clarity that are, indeed, stunning.

Still, nothing more had come of these early "scribbles,"

as she called them, and she wondered if it ever would. Our conversations were punctuated by arresting insights, clearly the fruit of many years of her reflections. Yet they were discrete, spontaneous moments that she had not been able to organize into something more. Even memories had become elusive when she worked at remembering alone. This was the first time that she said to me that remembering required conversation "fully to bring it out."

Without directly saying so, the survivor-diarist and the interviewer-psychologist were recruiting each other for a project that would extend over more than two decades. Later, you will read Agi's reflections about our work together. On one side, she concludes that, paradoxically, it was precisely all the experiences we did *not* share that made our collaboration possible. "Nothing was presumed. Nothing was taken for granted," she notes. "And that provided both of us the time and space to learn about it, and reflect upon it, together." At the same moment, what we did share was equally essential. Agi calls us "mind readers": "The longer we worked, the deeper our friendship and our collaboration became. Somehow, we developed a rapport that even now, after twenty-five years, I don't think we understand." Indeed, we don't understand it; except that it, too, made everything else possible.

The particulars of how we worked together are important, both to fully understand the form and evolution of *Reflections* and because the process of our collaboration speaks to wider questions about Holocaust memory and its transmission. But an Introduction can only do so much. So I have included a section,

"Notes on Co-authorship," at the end of these pages for readers who are interested in that level of detail and its implications.

Here, I would only add this: a book about the Holocaust is inevitably about loss and deprivation, irremediably so. But *Reflections* is also about nurture and human connection. Only they make possible, to the extent anything makes possible, life's recreation. That is what I have learned through all my years of conversation with Agi. And that is also what I have received.

—Henry Greenspan

REFLECTIONS

REFLECTIONS

The Looking Glass

SOME YEARS AGO, a new collection of photographs from Auschwitz was published. It is strange enough to think of these as "coffee table" books, but that is what some of them resemble. Oversized volumes, full of pictures from a place where "coffee" itself was a euphemism for the dark bitter drink they passed out to us each morning.

This particular book contained photos that had been found by a survivor. It is not certain who took them; most likely one of the guards. Nor is it clear why they were taken. One story has it that photography was simply the guard's hobby.

I had looked through the book once and found an uncle of mine. That was all I noticed. Then a woman, another survivor, called from New York. She had recognized herself in one of the photos and said that I was there as well.

I cannot tell you that I immediately went to look. I was curious. And I was not curious. And when I finally did see it? I was simply stunned that such a photo existed. I was stunned to see myself, there and then.

I don't remember anyone taking photos of us at the time. And seeing the picture didn't bring back any other memories either. Really, it led nowhere. It was just that frozen moment. It was less like looking in a mirror than looking *through* a mirror—to some dark shadow land on the other side, where I am looking back.

This is not surprising. Photos are the outsider's way of remembering Auschwitz, but they are not ours. From the inside, we remember smells—the stench of the camp, the odor of unwashed flesh, the odor of burning flesh. And sounds—screaming, beatings, pleading, the whistle of a whip or of a train. We remember the feelings of exhaustion and hunger and helplessness and cold. And the feeling of having no feeling. But seeing, if we let ourselves see at all, was done mostly through averted eyes. Our memories of Auschwitz do not have the objectivity of photographs. We were rarely so shameless or so bold.

Still, I return to the book every now and then. I cannot tell you why. Am I still searching for something? Trying to remember something? I don't think so. I simply look to look. She is still there. She has not disappeared. And the others too, the ones in so many of the other photos, are also still there, in those brief last moments when they had their pictures taken.

Almost none of them made it to the other side of the mirror. They do not own coffee tables. They do not pursue hobbies. They are only in the dark photos, stopped cold. And they are in those ragged, fragile albums that we carry in our memories and in our dreams.

Photograph from *The Auschwitz Album*. From the left, Agi is the second woman from the outside of the second full row, face deep in shadows, kerchief appearing checkered.

A DREAM OF
MUNKACS

Boundaries

I WAS BORN in a little city that is called Munkacs in Hungarian and Mukačevo in Czech. The town is near the border and has gone back and forth between the two countries over the years. So I am sometimes from Czechoslovakia and sometimes from Hungary. As you will hear, the boundaries of my world have changed many times.

But Munkacs was my childhood, and I remember it as a warm, fun-loving city. Before the war, it was 40 percent Jewish, and people from the surrounding area came because we had the only Hebrew high school, the *gymnasium*. I myself was too young for the *gymnasium* and went to the Hebrew elementary school until 1939. In that year, Hitler seized the western part of Czechoslovakia and divided up the rest. Hungary, allied with Germany, took over the part of Czechoslovakia that had included Munkacs. One of the first things the Hungarians did was to close our school. It was not only us. They shut down all but the Hungarian schools, so the Russian and Czech schools disappeared as well.

Still, daily life did not yet change dramatically. Being Jewish, keeping the Sabbath, gathering with family were its foundation. Beyond that, for children, life was to study, to play, and to swim in the River Latorca that passed through our town. My best friend was Marika, whom I had known since kindergarten. I saw her every day because her house was on the way to school. We walked there together.

There was a big chestnut tree in her family's backyard, and this was our meeting place where we talked, made our plans, shared our dreams. She had an older sister, I had a younger brother, and there was also Bela, my handsome older cousin. There was plenty to discuss.

If Marika and I had a fight, we would find a third party to act as mediator. We talked through our "middleman." "You tell Agi that I said so and so." And I would say back, to the mediator, "You tell Marika this and such." And so we never stopped talking, even if we sometimes needed the diplomatic go-between to help us make peace.

Marika's house was in the middle of the city, near the Korzo, the promenade where people strolled and socialized. For us, this was a scene of constant interest—who was walking with whom, whom we would see, and whom we might meet. One evening we were out later than was usual for kids our age, and we ran into one of our teachers—an enormous man who somehow always terrified us. When we saw him, we ran in the other direction. Later, when we thought it was safe, we ran back out—and practically into his arms. "You little lambs, what are you running from?" We didn't answer. We just turned and ran back to Marika's house as fast as we could.

Our homework that night was to memorize a poem by Bialik for his class. "The Bird"—I still remember it. But I did not remember a single line of it when our teacher called on me the next day, and neither did Marika. Such was the power of our fear! And such is the power of memory that holds on to these fragments—the normal fears, the normal times—just as Marika and I would try to hold on to each other even in the midst of all boundaries tearing apart.

Hebrew elementary school of Munkacs, late 1930s. Agi is in middle row (third up from the front), sixth from the left. Marika is third from the left in the same row.

Rumors

Until 1939, when the Hungarians took over Munkacs, we lived side by side with our non-Jewish neighbors and there never seemed to be serious problems. They accepted who we were; we accepted who they were. Slowly, things began to change.

For the year after the Hebrew elementary school was closed, I went to a Hungarian school. My mother had a friend who was a teacher there. The next year, part of the old *gymnasium* was reorganized into a Hebrew girls' school. My friends and I attended it until 1944.

Many of the Czechs were simply driven out of town. My

father felt loyal to them, and we moved to a part of the city that some thought might remain Czech, although that did not happen. Then, in 1942, the Hungarians took almost all the Jewish men into forced labor. That included my father. He could come back sometimes, on the weekends, but essentially he was no longer with us from that time.

My mother was constantly worried about him. She tried to send things or visit, and a few times we came along. My Aunt Olga, my mother's sister, moved in with us because her husband was also taken. Now our family itself had changed.

We heard only a little of what was going on outside of Hungary, and, as a kid, I didn't understand politics. I remember hearing with one ear that some Polish Jews had arrived in our town. A man was telling horror stories about people being killed in large numbers; he said that he himself had escaped from a mass grave. Nobody believed him. We thought he was either crazy or wanted sympathy. So people helped him out, fed him, pitied him, and sent him on his way. And, of course, I remembered this years later, when we had our own unbelievable stories to tell.

My own turning point was also my little brother's, who was six years old when the Germans, now distrusting their Hungarian allies, occupied the country in 1944. My brother was a sweet, smart, trusting little boy who had a good friend in Munkacs— Laci, the town drunk! Years before, Laci had been shot and lost one of his legs. People took care of him as they could.

My brother, Miki, was his real friend. He would find Laci

lying in the street, and help him get up. He took food out of the house without telling my mother why. "I'm hungry. I need a sandwich." He put it in his pocket and brought it to Laci.

One day Miki came in crying. "Mother, smell me!" he said. She said, "Yes, Mikike, what is it?"

"Do I stink?"

"Of course not!"

"Well then how come Laci called me a 'dirty, stinking Jew'? He is my friend."

Miki had tried to help him off the ground, and Laci shoved him away. "Go away, you dirty Jew." Little did he know that this was his destiny—that as a Jew, at the age of six, Miki would be shoved and pushed and cremated a few months later.

The Brick Factory

THE GERMANS CAME at holiday time—it was Passover, 1944, when they marched into Munkacs. Now things happened quickly. Schools were closed. We had to wear the yellow star. A small ghetto of two or three streets was created. Many had to move. For a brief time, a German officer lived in our own home. He was friendly and polite, our holiday guest.

After two weeks, most of the Jewish families were forced to pack up—we were allowed five kilos—and we were marched to a brick factory on the outskirts of the city. For a month this was our home. We slept outside, under the stars, trying to create whatever protection and privacy we could. We used the bricks themselves, piling them together, to make a kind of fence. My aunt found an old sled that we turned into a shelter. We still had some of our own bedding. We held on to each other.

We almost got used to it. I remember we young people throwing bricks from one to the other as part of a work team. My mother said, "If you can throw bricks here, you can go to Palestine and build things there. You can build a new country when all of this is finished. I will let you go." My mother was not an ardent Zionist. But she must have already realized that our life in Munkacs was over.

One day a young neighbor, a Ukrainian Christian boy, came up to the fence around the factory. Our families had been neighbors; he and I had been playmates. He used to play the harmonica and serenade me. I don't recall his expression or exactly what he said; only that he came and was looking at us through the fence. I was not happy to see him, and I called out: "What did you come for? To pity us? We don't need your pity. We don't want it." Looking back, I don't know why he came. Perhaps it was pity. Perhaps he was actually trying to help. Perhaps he was saying good-bye, a last serenade.

Whatever it was, he was the only one who came. From all of the town of Munkacs, that was sometimes Mukačevo, he was the only intentional witness.

Cattle Car

"PACK! YOU ARE going to a place to work." In the dark of night, we were put in the cattle cars.

The car was filled beyond capacity—no toilet, no privacy, no food, no water. Some people became hysterical. I remember their screams. Out of so much horror and pain, it is perhaps surprising that the sounds of screaming—then and later—are among the worst memories of all.

Mostly, though, I remember our own little corner—my mother, my aunt, my six-year-old brother, and myself. My mother was concerned about my father, whom we had not seen in many months. And she was watching over me. "I hope you won't be too hungry. I know you get headaches. I hope you won't go hungry for too long." She knew that I could barely manage hunger. In fact, I was terribly scared, hungry, and thirsty. And yet I felt secure within this protected corner. Amidst the screams and the misery, I retreated into my mother's care. I drew from it everything I could.

I don't remember much more—three days, four days—and then the train came to a halt. The end of one life. The beginning of something else.

NIGHTMARE

The Crazy Unit

THE DOOR OPENS. "Out! Out! Fast! Fast!" Germans screaming. Mothers are holding on to their babies. Younger people are holding on to the elderly. Everyone is ordered to line up in rows of five. "Push! Push! Fast! Fast!" There is no time to orient yourself. And around us the people with shaved heads and striped clothes, running, rushing, everywhere. "This must be the crazy unit," I think to myself. "This must be the insane asylum."

The chaos becomes a line. I am in front of a tall German officer, looking down, pointing, left, right. His finger sends me to the left—I am the only one from my row sent to the left. My mother, my little brother, and my aunt are all on the right. I don't want to be alone. I am fifteen years old, and I want to be with my family. I run over to where they are. The finger forces me back—to the left, to the left. I try it again. I try it a third time because they are moving away. This time I am thrown hard to the gravel. I look at my mother, pleading. She is going away, and she sees me being thrown to the ground.

She waves her hand. "Go, my child, go. We will see each other tomorrow."

And I have been going ever since then.

Striped Clothes

Our heads were shaved. Our clothes were taken. We were sent through a shower and, on the other side, we were given striped uniforms. Somehow, I managed to retrieve a good pair of shoes from the pile that had been pushed to one side. They were well made, more like boots than shoes, and I would wear them throughout the year to come. Extraordinary luck; they were my own.

I was alone. We were led into a large barracks, one very large room, like a warehouse. All of us who had been sent to the left were there. With shaved heads and striped clothes, we had also become the "crazy unit." People were milling around, confused, uncertain. It was still the same night.

I was numb and in a kind of daze, wandering through the room. Without realizing it, I was calling out my girlfriend's name. "Marika. Marika." I had not seen her since the brick factory, but I must have guessed she was here. And, strangely enough, she was also wandering about, calling out for me. As it turned out, we had already walked past each other. Without hair, in these clothes, we needed voice first. Toward dawn, I heard my name.

"Agi. Agi." There she was. We stared at each other. Head shaved. Striped clothes. The moment of recognition. And what did we do? We laughed! Hysterically. "How *awful* you look, Agika!" she chided. "How awful *you* look, Marika!" We were still kids. We had no idea how we looked until we saw each other. My face, my own bald head, was reflected in hers; and in her astonished eyes.

Shortly, we would be tattooed. I would become A6013. People were being murdered all around us. There was the smell, the screams, the flames. We didn't know everything, but we knew enough. Still, we laughed. Because we were still kids who thought we looked very silly standing in an insane asylum with no hair and striped clothes.

Slices

CHAOS, RUNNING, SCREAMING, sickness, stench, dogs barking, guards barking, beating, whipping, pushed and pushed. *Zehlappel*—endless roll calls, day and night. They are big. We are tiny. They are monstrous. We are kids.

They take us from the warehouse barracks to the A-Lager, the main camp of Auschwitz. Our beds are narrow shelves, each with six people. If you are small enough, you can barely sleep on one side. Our food is black bread, hard as a brick, that I didn't recognize at first as food. I wanted to throw it away, but I was afraid I would be punished if I did. So I simply hid it some-

where. No doubt some lucky person found it; someone who
already knew that little brick was life itself.

Clothes, hair, names, food—they took everything. And so,
in a way, we adopted each other. Marika was still with her older
sister and her mother, and the four of us made a family together. We comforted each other, we tried to align ourselves in the
bunk to make more room, we cooked imaginary meals for each
other that we enjoyed in imaginary lives. Chicken paprikash, my
favorite! With lots of bread, a big round *challah* in the middle of
the table. We said that after the war we would always keep a loaf
of bread like that, the eternal centerpiece of our hungry lives,
and we would be able to take some anytime we wanted. It would
always be there. But meanwhile maybe we can make this little
black brick last one day. In the meantime, maybe we can make
paper-thin slices. Maybe we can slice the paper-thin slices. And
maybe there are crumbs. Maybe there is dust.

Adoption

BEFORE AUSCHWITZ, MARIKA's mother was simply Marika's mother to me. She was always kind, refined, and well dressed, small in stature, delicate in style. She had a very light complexion that set off striking, pitch-black hair. She reminded me of a porcelain doll. She was thirty-six when we were taken to Auschwitz, but she already had started to age. She had had a dream, a premonition, of much of what would happen. She sensed that her husband was already dead, which turned out to be true. When her hair started to grow in, it came back entirely white.

I can't say precisely why, but I took it as my purpose to keep her alive and bring her home. It was a kind of vow, and it gave me strength. I had someone to care for, and that was much easier than simply caring for myself. I was not being generous. I was giving myself a purpose and a responsibility. When everything else is taken, still having a responsibility is not a trivial thing.

It was mutual. Marika's mother talked about the future whether she believed in it or not: what we would do, what she would cook for us. She tried to give us strength, and we tried to give it back to her.

In Auschwitz, everyone had their masquerade—the killers, too. They had their orchestras, their shower rooms, their *arbeit macht frei*. And we had our mothers, our sisters, our big round bread. It was a crazy unit through and through.

Animals

A<small>FTER A COUPLE</small> of weeks, we were ready to begin our work. The four of us were assigned to what was called the "white kerchief" commando; that was what we wore. Every day we were marched from A-Lager to B-Lager, Auschwitz-Birkenau. In a month we would stay there permanently, but at this point the new barracks were still being built. Birkenau was the part of Auschwitz where they had the large gas chambers and the crematoria; Birkenau was where they did most of the killing. Our work was to sort the clothes of those who had already been gassed and burned.

We passed the crematoria every day. We worked nearby. I remember the strange quietness that came over us when we walked by.

Did we know? People went in; they didn't come out. We saw the lines from the transports. Only smoke and flames came out. And everywhere the smell of burning flesh. I said to myself, "No. That's *not* my mother. That's *not* my brother. That's *not* my family."

Did we know? Of course we knew. How could we not know? Did we know? Of course we didn't know. How could we let ourselves know?

I remember one day I decided I was an animal. I said to myself: "You fool. What are you trying to do? This is the end of the world. You are not a human being. Because here people are being killed by the thousands. More are arriving. There is smoke coming out of the chimney. Everywhere the smell. And you are going on? You are still here? You are hungry? Only an animal could endure this. God killed all the human beings, and only the animals are left."

I accepted my own verdict: I was no longer a human being. There was a certain relief. I didn't have to prove anything anymore. I was an animal, beaten, numb, and dumb. And yet, in all the little ways, I rebelled—taking care of our camp mother, deciding I had a purpose, comforting another prisoner as she was dying. Resignation brought defiance; it brought a stubborn anger.

Is this hope? Is it strength? Is it vanity? I will have more to say about vanity.

The Elite Crew

AFTER A MONTH, we were moved into the new barracks at Birkenau, and this was where we stayed until the evacuation of the camp in January 1945. Our work continued to be sorting the belongings of those who arrived from the transports. There were different piles for clothing, jewelry, shoes—mountains of things, all of it packed up and sent to Germany. Every few days, a truck came and took it away. But there was always more; the destruction of the Hungarian Jews was fully under way.

We were known as the "elite crew"—I'm not sure why. Working inside, at least much of the time, made it easier. We also had some access to food that we found among the clothes. And, of course, we were "on the inside" of the killing process. We knew what was going on whether we wanted to know or not. We saw the people coming in and not going out. We sent their clothes on without them.

There were two Germans guarding our barracks, but they were not always on the inside. We had our own watchmen to warn us when they were coming, and we had a password, *geshem,* which is Hebrew for "rain." When we heard it, we sped up, looking as efficient as possible, working as hard as we could. Otherwise, we found small ways to sabotage—cutting up clothes, shredding what we could, hoping they would be less useful in the Reich. I don't know if this hurt them, but doing it helped us.

Every now and then, remnants of our own lives passed through our hands. One day I found the coat of my aunt who had been on the transport with us. I wanted to keep it, but there was no way that I could. And then I found a photo of my cousin Bela that I hid in my shoe. It quickly became discolored, the image was completely worn away, but I held on to it until not a single bit remained—only white powder. And one day I found a jacket that looked like my own jacket. I didn't believe it; anybody could have a white jacket. But then I reached into the pocket and found a piece of paper. It was from school, some notes about a Hebrew presentation I had to make. They probably wouldn't find much use for my homework in Germany. I cut the coat to shreds.

Passing Through

Every now and then, remnants of our lives passed through our hands. In our dreams and in our small camp family and in fragments of a photograph, we held on to stray bits of memory.

One day, I learned that an aunt of mine, my father's sister, would be coming through our camp. She was being kept in another part of Auschwitz but was temporarily assigned to a work group whose job it was to haul away the excrement from our own section of the camp. Somehow, we each knew the other was in Auschwitz, but we had not seen each other since home.

As her group passed through, I rushed up to her when I thought the guard wasn't looking. It was only a moment, an exchange of looks, a touch.

Even that was too long. It turned out that one of the guards had seen me. As punishment, I was made to kneel on the gravel in front of our barracks. I had to stay that way for twenty-four hours. I was to be an example, as though, across from the crematoria, we needed more examples. It rained part of the night. I remember the rain was soothing.

It turns out that my Aunt Goldie also survived. When we met after the war, she told me that she had had a dream in which her father told her that she was going to make it home. He himself had died in 1938, before the war began. The dream was her own talisman. In those brief moments, her father had come back. Even there, she imagined, he was passing through.

Garbage

T HE WIDER SCENE, the constant murder, was out of our control. It was only yards from where we worked, but, horrible as this may sound, it became a kind of background. We tried to block it out, and we focused on what was more immediate—the bread, the shreds, and the dear ones that were still within our grasp or within our dreams.

I had a friend, someone from Munkacs, who was one of the twins who were being kept alive for medical experiments. One day, I saw him on the other side of the wires. I was able to throw some of the food we were sorting over the fence for him and for his sister, and as soon as he got it, he ran. I turned to find an SS *Hauptscharfuhrer* standing behind me, along with a little female kapo. The kapo slapped me hard twice, probably to impress the officer with what a good kapo she was. The *Hauptscharfuhrer* smirked at the sight. Then he looked down at me and said, in effect, "Okay, if you have the guts to come here and do this, then maybe you don't need to be killed." But this time my punishment was that I was no longer allowed to work inside, sorting the goods and clothes. I was put to work in the garbage area, outdoors, instead.

The nights were becoming colder. But in the garbage I was able to find some potato peelings. And over a little candle I cooked soup that I brought to our camp mother, who was failing more and more. This was hot food, which is what I thought she needed. Crazy or not, oblivious or not, we did what we could with the garbage where they tossed us.

Scheisskapos

ANOTHER STORY ABOUT doing what you can:

During the time I was working outside, I saw another prisoner who had been given the title, *Scheisskapo*. I remember she had wavy dark hair—her head wasn't shaved—and she was pudgy and pretty, with an agreeable disposition.

Scheisskapo means "the shit commander." It was written on a sign she had to wear around her neck. Her job was to stand all day in the prisoners' latrine—a long bench with a row of holes over a pit filled with quicklime. Her job was to be a kind of attendant, to tell you when you could come in and when you had to leave, to keep it neat and clean.

One day I saw that this woman, the *Scheisskapo*, had found a couple of old boxes, a large wooden crate and a smaller one. She also had a little mirror that she probably found among the clothes of those who had been killed. She put the largest box against the wall and put the mirror on top of it. And she put the smaller box in front, where she could sit. So with the boxes and the mirror she made a little vanity, a little vanity in the corner of the ladies' room.

I must say that I admired what she had done. She had improvised her own little world, even in Birkenau. That may, indeed, have been the best you could do there—be a *Scheisskapo* sitting at your vanity in your own little corner of the latrine.

Screaming

We did what we could, and everyone did it their own way. Some made small families and tried to stay together. Some dreamed and pretended. Some became selfish or vicious, stealing from each other and fighting with each other at every turn. Others became hysterical, unable to contain their terror or their grief.

During the summer of 1944, people were being killed by the thousands every day in Birkenau. The crematoria were so busy that they made a special waiting barracks where they put people before they could destroy them. This was directly across from our barracks.

One night one of our kapos, whose name was Manci, found out that her sister and her sister's small child had been brought to the camp. They were in the waiting barracks. Somehow, Manci talked the Germans into getting her sister out, and this woman stayed in our barracks that night. Her child was left behind.

When the woman realized that her child was doomed, she started to scream. "I want my child! I want my child!" She began to beat on her sister: "Why did you save my life? Why did you bring me here! I want my child! I want my child!" She went completely berserk, the entire night, and her screaming was driving all of us berserk as well. These are the things that you cannot push away no matter how hard you try. The sights of horror you can somehow block out. But the screams bore into you.

They stay. I remember an earlier night in July when they killed everyone in the "family camp" as they called it, which was where they put the Jews who had been deported from Theresienstadt. These people knew what was coming; they had been in Birkenau long enough to know it very well.

I will never forget the sounds. There was screaming. There was singing, *Ani Maamim,* "I believe in the coming of the Messiah." There were shouts of farewell—parents saying good-bye to children, old people saying good-bye to their families, a whole community saying good-bye to life. The *Sh'ma,* "Hear, O Israel." The end of the *Sh'ma.* The end of everything. Silence screaming just as loud.

I will never forget these sounds. They will always haunt me.

Hear, O Israel.

Deserters

THERE WERE DIFFERENT ways to try to resist, and different weapons. We knew one man, a friend of ours who had been a doctor in Munkacs, who became a member of the *Sonderkommando* in Birkenau. These were the prisoners who worked inside the crematoria. Their job was to remove the dead after the gassings and load the corpses into the ovens.

One day we talked with him through the wires that separated our group from theirs. He said to me, "We have it too good. We are being well fed. We sleep on silk sheets. This means the end for us. They are fattening us up for the kill. But they are not going to gas us." I later realized that he was referring to the *Sonderkommando's* plan to set off an explosion in one of the crematoria. Just then a German approached, and he went away.

The next day we were awakened by gunshots. At *Zehlappel* they made us march to the crematorium. The *Sonderkommando* had all been shot. They were lying face up so we could see their looks of horror, and among them was our friend.

"This is what happens to deserters," the Germans barked. That's what they called them: "deserters."

I suppose they were.

Dreams

As a result of the explosion, one of the crematoria stopped working, but it didn't make much difference. This was already October 1944. The great mass of people had already been destroyed. And the Germans had a hundred other ways to kill us, as we witnessed all the time.

In the midst of such terror, life became more and more narrow. The flames are real. That's where all the people from the family camp went. That's where our own families went. That's where we will go as well. You try to pull the shade, you try to block it out, but you are never really successful. It gets inside.

And it stays inside.

Like my aunt, I also had a recurring dream during the time I was in Auschwitz. It always came and went the same way. I was sitting in my mother's lap. She was there, and I was trying, once more, to burrow into her corner of protection. But, at the same moment, the fence of Auschwitz was also there, the barbed wire. And that's how the dream always ended—with the image of the fence. The good, sheltered feeling was fragile. Even in a dream, its boundaries were invaded every time. It was as much as I could salvage.

"Go, my child, go," my mother waved her hand. "We will see each other tomorrow."

DEATH MARCH
AND WAKING

Blood

In January 1945 the Germans evacuated most of the prisoners still alive in Auschwitz. The Soviet army was advancing from the east, and the camp itself would soon be liberated. For most of us, though, freedom was still months away. Indeed, for most of us, January 1945 signaled nothing more than another way to die. This was the beginning of the death marches in which people were killed as readily by freezing and shooting as by gas. Those who persisted in living were marched through the winter and concentrated in camps farther and farther inside the German fatherland—places like Ravensbruck, Bergen-Belsen, or Dachau, where so much of the nightmare had begun.

For us, it began with blood. The German army needed blood—even our poison Jewish blood—and they selected anyone who looked like they could give. For the first time, I was separated from my camp family, and that was terrifying. In fact, one of the sisters was with me at first, but I sent her back so she could be with her own, real family. I was alone and was drained of as much blood as could be taken. We were, in essence, blood cattle: they gave us a bit more to eat, and then they milked us. I could hardly stand up when it was done.

Soon after the blood-drawing, everyone was lined up in rows and the evacuations began. I was able to get back to my group, and this again made all the difference. During the march we supported each other—literally. While three walked, one slept, being dragged along by the others. We took turns, walking and sleeping.

Ahead of us was the men's group, and we constantly passed the dead bodies, and wounded bodies, of those who had been shot. They had strayed, exhausted, from the line or were too weak to line up in the first place. The half-dead were more horrifying than the dead. Wounded, bleeding, they raised their heads or arms. They called out to us: "Help me! Take me with you!" And there was nothing we could do. We continued to walk. Once again, I comforted myself with the thought that only the animals had been spared. And the Germans, pumping our animal blood.

Fathers

W E DRANK SNOW, ate snow, slept in snow. We were still in our striped clothes, but I had a sweater underneath that I got from the sorting. And shoes that were much too large. And a kerchief. And no socks.

The air raids provided breaks, and we welcomed them. The bombs rained down around us, but we were delighted, screaming with joy in the middle of the attack. "They are coming; the liberators are coming, whatever happens to us." Later on, I became delirious. I was completely gone and hallucinating. I was thinking that my father was coming to save me, because I still thought of my father as a soldier, someone in the forced labor battalion. I saw him in all the trucks that went by and among the soldiers who were guarding us. "There is my father. My father is coming."

One of the soldiers was about to shoot me for wandering toward him out of the line. Someone pulled me back and shoved a piece of sugar in my mouth. Somehow I regained energy. They hid me in the line, and we went on walking.

Ravensbruck

THE FIRST SIGNIFICANT stop was Ravensbruck, the real nightmare, a nightmare I had for many years and still today. The barbed
wire, the hanging trees, they seemed to be symbolic of the end of
the world. Ravensbruck was the pit of pits, a camp of the camps,
because it was a collection point for all the prisoners from the east.
Thousands of people were concentrated in a few barracks, dying
of work, hunger, or just giving up. We were all sick. We were all
exhausted and delirious.

But how to explain this? Even at the end of the world, there
were times...

We were lined up once, to get food they told us, which turned out not to be true. Marika was ahead of me. And I saw, just as she turned around, she got hit in the head by a whip. And I said, "Don't cry, Marika! In a minute, I'll get it too!" And in a split second, before I even stopped talking, the whip did get me too. It was terribly painful. But as soon as the whip hit me, the two of us broke into laughter, such laughter that people thought we were completely crazy. We still laugh about it—"It will get me too, and *crack!*" We don't talk about the reality of the camp. Ravensbruck, the pit of pits, is reduced to this one idiotic thing.

If it weren't for such idiotic things, we would have been dead long before.

Lice

The pit of pits led to more marching, and later to Malchov, which was, in some ways, even worse. The floors were covered with straw, and the straw was covered with lice. There was no escape from them. We met an older woman from Munkacs and her daughter, and, incredibly fortunate for us, they were able to get us clean clothes. But as soon as we sat or lay down, we were covered by lice again.

Malchov was a waiting place for death, and death was crawling by the millions on the floor. Malchov was a lice factory, and it was the end even of the little purpose we had been able, at times, to salvage. When you are covered with lice, filthy, itching everywhere, driving you insane, there is no purpose but relief, but cessation. Even now, so many years later, I cannot tolerate insects. If a fly comes into the room, I go crazy.

I could not have endured this any longer than I did. I am certain I could not have made it. And once you are covered with lice, you are never completely free of them. Skin has memory. No, skin *is* memory. And you can never shed its crawling and its many grasping mouths.

The Fortune Teller

MALCHOV FORETOLD ONLY death, and yet not quite. We met, of all things, a fortune teller there, a French woman, one of the prisoners. She sat in that place and predicted the future. She helped people believe, not in their own future, but in the idea of the future itself.

I remember her intensity, her eyes. And yet there was a gentle kindness about her. She read palms, and she told me that I would get out, that I will survive. But she also said that our camp mother, who was failing badly, would not make it.

Between Ravensbruck and Malchov we had been briefly

transported by train. Stopped at a station one night, the train was bombed by Allied planes. The next day, emerging from the cattle car, we saw that the train and its cargo—other prisoners from the march—had been almost entirely destroyed. Only our car and part of another were still intact. There were pieces of train and pieces of people everywhere.

Do such experiences, such arbitrary chances, help or hinder the fortune tellers? Even today, I am not sure.

A Diary

After Malchov, we were again on the march, but it was evident that the end was coming even if we did not know how or when. The planes flew lower, just over our heads. We could even see the pilots, seeing us. We could hear the artillery behind us. The German guards wore civilian clothes to avoid being taken as soldiers. They were clearly preparing for defeat; some had already scattered. Yet when people from the march stopped to get some water, or gather twigs for a small fire, or were too exhausted to go on, there was still time for killing.

Toward the very end, our line of prisoners was led into a

dark forest. My camp mother was slipping further and further; it was evident she was dying. It was also clear to us, my camp sisters and I, that if we had come this far together, we would die together too. We could not go on. We left the line along with a few others who were unable to continue, and we began to say good-bye to life. I didn't know then if my father was still alive, but I needed to believe he was. I also needed to apologize to him that I would not be coming home. The transport moved on, without us.

As it turned out, our liberation was only a few days off. As I will describe, in late April 1945 we were taken to what had been a prisoner-of-war camp, a *stalag* that was made up mostly of Allied soldiers whom the Germans had captured on Crete. We were soon to find ourselves in the camp hospital, surrounded by a care that we could hardly still imagine.

In the hospital, I began to write about the events that we had just experienced, and were still experiencing, even as I was writing. I am not sure what compelled me, although an instinct to record seemed to be one of the first things to return as life itself began to return. I started my account with our last day on the death march and the final fate of our camp mother, whom I call "my lady" in these pages.

The entries were originally written in Hungarian. The first date, April 20, 1945, was a couple of days before my writing itself began.

April 20, 1945

We are surrounded by flames. Our liberators are coming. And our enemies are also approaching. So we, forsaken, tired, and hungry, are walking toward liberation. The marching mass, the long line of the transport, drags itself along. It moves slowly and painfully, on and on.

I see only four people. A dying woman who still wants to live, her two daughters, and myself. We surround the dying one and we are begging her to look at us. She must go on. She wants to continue, but she falls back. Her strength is gone. She cannot move. There is nothing to do. We are not going either. Let them shoot us. That is all we can expect from the German masters.

I look around: flames, terrible screams, are coming from the line. I look up at the sky. And I call for my father who is suffering somewhere in Russia. "Help me, Father. You are the only one left. Only you are waiting for me. I still have to live for your sake." I receive no answer. Only dying words.

Delirious, I even turn to the guards: "Officer, officer! Sir, if you know God a little bit, bring me a little wagon for the dying one. With a wagon maybe I will be able to save a life."

No answer. They pass me by. There is no wagon.

Suddenly I have an idea. I grab my lady and start

pulling her along. "Let's run. Let's take her away. Let's save her. The liberators are here. She has to live!" We aren't able to carry her very far.

She falls down. And the three of us remain standing. Now we wait for the end. I don't want to leave them. And the countless rows, the dark rows, pass us by.

Someone among them calls out to me: "Come with us! You can see they are barely alive. You are strong. You can still work. You cannot stay with them. Come with us."

They are tempting me. I turn around and look at my threesome. Maybe I should go to my father, to my liberators. But still no. Something is telling me that I should stay. No, I'm not going to leave them. I grab my girlfriends. We hug each other and cry bitterly under the sky. This is how we remain together.

A miracle. A flatbed truck does arrive and they throw us in it. The truck takes us farther and farther away, and we leave the transport behind. God Almighty, a miracle has happened! We are sitting together. And sitting up, we soon fall asleep.

As in a dream, I hear that the mother doesn't live anymore. I wake up. But then we say, "Let it be." Either way, we know that this is the end.

So we fall into a very deep sleep. Neither the flames around us nor the liberation interests us, because that is all impossible. We don't care anymore. We don't even notice who else is on the truck and how we are escaping from the Germans. I'm sleeping because I haven't slept for weeks. And I'm sleeping because I'm out of my senses. And I'm sleeping because I don't want to be aware of anything.

We come to a sudden stop, and they throw us out of the truck. The truck has accomplished its task. It turns around and disappears.

An elderly German man, a civilian, receives us. He listens to our suffering, about the starvation and the misery. We three introduce ourselves as the dead woman's daughters, and the German is almost fatherly toward us. We surround the dead one, who lies on the ground.

We want to speak with her, but no words come out. I stare at the ground until I am shoved in the back by a German guard. "Remove that corpse immediately!" I look at him in bewilderment. I don't move. He hits me hard across the face.

Dizzy, hysterical, I fall to the ground. I get up, still disoriented. The old German consoles me. He says to the guard that he shouldn't hurt me.

We found a piece of potato that had been in her pocket. And we ate it. Don't be surprised—we were starving.

Later they brought a few stretchers for the severely wounded ones who were also on the truck. We have to move on again. I bent down to the dead mother, very close to her, and I asked her forgiveness. I wanted to pray but I couldn't. All that was left was tears.

We kissed her and left her in a ditch. We went on with the heavy stretchers, on and on. We wanted to get to somewhere warm, wherever that could be.

Surprise—we arrive at a barn that is filled with hay. Without thinking, we throw ourselves down on it. There are no words and no thoughts within us. In a moment we are all in a deep sleep. Let's dream, let's forget. This day has brought enough.

Prisoners-of-War

LIBERATION CAME IN steps, and the next day it stepped closer. We began to meet the soldiers who were really in charge of the camp: British, French, Belgians, Yugoslavs, and more. Apparently they had an understanding with the Germans that they would take over as the *Wehrmacht* withdrew before the Soviet advance, and this next day was the start of the transition. The barn where we had been left was adjacent to the camp itself.

The Allied soldiers had heard of the death camps, but we were the first people they had seen who had been there. And, notwithstanding all the combat they had experienced, seeing us—we girl-skeletons from Auschwitz—somehow overwhelmed them. As they led us from the barn, into the camp, and on to the hospital, they formed a kind of spontaneous honor guard. By the time we reached the hospital, there were literally two rows of soldiers, one on each side of us, which was their way of welcoming us and paying respect to what they sensed we had endured. Their responsiveness was genuine, and their care and compassion were extraordinary.

As my diary makes clear, while describing our last hours in the barn and then our move to the hospital, it took a while for us to believe that we were truly safe—that the bread would be there tomorrow, that the hospital was really a hospital. Still, looking back, I am surprised that we could feel so quickly that we belonged to the world again. It was because these good men, our liberators, were the world that welcomed us.

April 21, 1945

We get up and look around the room. And soon we meet our companions in the barn. They are Hungarians, Poles, Russians, French. They do not make a very good first impression on me.

The sun comes in. Food is arriving. Bread, margarine, and black coffee—things that we haven't seen in many weeks. To us, this is a fairy tale, a Cinderella story. We could have eaten all the bread. There was enough to fill us. But we didn't dare. "What will happen tomorrow?" We look at it and put it aside.

As the healthiest among us three, I go to work. I bring water and wash the sick ones. The morning goes by quickly. Sleeping, eating, drinking coffee, washing ourselves for the first time in months. Noon comes and dinner arrives—a two-course meal! Soup and a potato. So we are kept busy. We are under shelter and getting food. But we are afraid of having to go back on the march. So we don't eat everything.

In the afternoon, we are surprised by a policeman at the window who speaks Hungarian. He had served in Germany. We spoke with him, and he promised to bring us milk in the evening. We are looking forward to that reunion. But he disappeared. We never saw him again.

There is dead silence in the room. Suddenly the door opens, and with the opening of this door we are brought back to our lives. A clean-cut officer enters whom I like immediately. And other officers too. An unusual sight—they are not Germans, yet they wear military uniforms. But these are our friends. They come in and bring smiles and contentment. We don't know who they are. We only know that they are good.

One bends down. But before he does, he looks like he is afraid of something. He says to us, *"Juden?"* Then he looks off to the side, and tries to hold back his tears.

He leaves the room, wipes his eyes, and returns.

With the kindest, most compassionate words, he tries to comfort us. He tells us that he has been a prisoner-of-war, a Jew. He and his comrades are going to take us to the hospital, which he says is a good place. But suddenly we are unsure. "A hospital? What is this? A trick?" All three of us answer in horror that we are healthy. We are afraid to go to this hospital. But the Jewish friend whose name we don't yet know stops the words in our mouths. "Don't be afraid. We are taking you to a good place. A place where we will take care of you."

Soon we gather ourselves and our belongings—a quarter of a bread and a potato. The wind is biting. We walk alongside this Jewish man. The rain that hits our faces almost raises our spirits. But they are still the faces of tired, broken prisoners, completely in a daze.

As we walk, I think of those from our transport still on the march—still being harassed, kicked, herded along. Suddenly a police car approaches us and stops. It goes on its way, and we continue our journey. Eventually, we come to the hospital.

In the courtyard, new faces greet us. These men look at us with astonishment. We are still in our dirty camp clothes, so it is not surprising that they are shocked by our appearance. We go down a hallway, into one of the rooms, where we are met by Frenchmen. We don't speak each other's languages, but we understand their kindness and compassion. Soon we are able to take warm showers and then to sink into bed. How good it feels!

The room fills with inquiring Frenchmen, Yugoslavs, British, and others of many nationalities. They are soldiers, former prisoners-of-war, who had not seen anyone like us before. They are interested in our fate. And when they leave, they bid good-bye with sadness and sensitivity in their eyes. They don't want to overly disturb us.

Now a bucketful of sweet milk arrives, and everyone can have as much as they want. And we don't have to stand in line for it! This didn't happen to us in the German camps. And now this has happened too!

Next, a very kind-looking French doctor comes in. He goes around and writes down everybody's ailment on his chart. Yes, we have come to experience this too!

I am here in a prisoner-of-war camp—me, as a woman, as a child. The American and English care packages come, and they provide what we need in the camp. After dinner, the doctor says good night. He wishes us rest and peace. "By tomorrow, not one German will remain here at the hospital. They will no longer rule over us at all!" We take his word for it and sink toward sleep. For the first time since I can't remember, we can stretch out on white sheets. We can rest. They are not going to wake us in the morning for the roll call, for the *Zehlappel.*

Marco

After a while, it became almost routine. The men would enter our room, take a look at us, and start to cry. And we, still not really understanding how we looked or what it meant to them to see us, began to giggle. One group would walk out; another would come in. We winked at each other: "They are going to cry again." And so they did. They cried, and we laughed.

For three months they cared for us, nurturing us back to life with food and milk and kindness. But the first man, the one who had asked us if we were Jewish, stands out among them all. This was Marco, who became a lifelong friend. He was our teacher and our guide—especially in those first crucial weeks. For us, it was like being born again. He was that little corner that I could only dream about in Auschwitz. My mother was gone and could not be replaced. But the memories of care and of belonging—the feelings themselves—were a foundation that could be built upon again.

Of course, there were other memories too, and they continued to rage within me in these first days of liberation and, I would learn, in all the years to come. That is what comes through in the next day's writing—the compulsion to remember and to retell; the wish for silence and for peace. It would be many years before I would learn that this dilemma has no resolution. It is a contradiction you live, not solve.

April 22, 1945

From out of a deep sleep we wake for breakfast. Hot tea is awaiting us. From the potatoes that remain, I fix a good puree that we spread over the bread. We still restrict ourselves to one slice of bread only. We may need the rest for tomorrow. But the biggest specialty at home wouldn't have tasted as good as this English tea and pureed potato. Hungry people appreciate anything that signifies food.

After breakfast, we get a very helpful visitor who brings us men's shirts and underwear. It doesn't matter—

it's clean. We are no longer scratching and always imagining the lice.

Many of the visitors' names we don't know. And there are so many. But among them is the Jewish man who brought us to this hospital. He takes the three of us as his sisters. His name is Marco Rubinovich, from Belgrade.

All the men are courteous and kind, but this one is special. His name we must write down, and even if we didn't we would remember. From his story, I learn that he went through some of the same suffering as we. He lost his family. But he himself didn't suffer as much because he was a prisoner-of-war and treated as a soldier through political arrangements. Thus he hadn't seen the Auschwitz crematoria, but only heard about them. Only through our stories did he learn what was done.

It's enough to listen to these horrors. The gas, the crematoria, the forced marches. It's enough to hear about it, let alone to have to see it. So that is enough of this for now.

Marco comes in very often and always arrives with news. "Be happy. Tomorrow, or the day after at the latest, we will be completely free. All the German dogs have left the hospital already. We are done with them. Brothers, sisters, rejoice!"

The poor man was wasting his breath trying to make us feel good. We still don't believe anything.

Up until the last moment, the crematorium is our nightmare. We are telling everybody about it, whether we want to or not. Our stories are only about the crematorium, whether we want to or not. Either in my dream or when I am awake, I only see the flames in front of me. And the vision never fades.

Too much talk tires us, so it's better for us to rest. The visitors are courteous. They would like to stay longer, but the doctor makes them leave.

So this is our new life. The day goes fast, and it is good. But now it is quiet. It's night. Let's sleep. Let's dream we shall be happy.

Liberation

THE NEXT DAY was the official liberation day—the arrival of the Russians. For us it was also the beginning of new questions: Where was home? What was home? What would we find there? And whom?

In some ways, this little hospital in no man's land had already become a home. We felt like comrades, and so we were. Some of the soldiers wanted to take us with them, and every time a group of them was transported home, after the liberation itself, they invited us along. "You come with us. You'll be a part of our family." They meant it. A Frenchman said, "I have two daughters.

We will have five daughters. I am a poor man. But we'll make do. Come, you will be our family."

There were enticements. But, in the end, there was really no question. We had to go home first, home to Munkacs, to see.

April 23, 1945 – The Liberation Day

There is a lot of commotion in the hallway. We wake up wondering—maybe it's our liberators? We don't wait very long because the men rush in with great joy. "The Russians are here! Rejoice! We are free! In a week or two, Germany will be completely kaput!"

Later on, a very high-ranking Russian officer and his retinue come in. Our friend Marco is with them as their interpreter. His face glows with happiness. He introduces us to the officer. We show him the number on our arms that we received in Auschwitz. The officer shakes his head. "This is unusual. There are very few."

This is not the way I pictured the liberation. It's not true. I don't believe it. "They can still take us back," I think to myself with fear. But I don't say anything out loud. The high-ranking officer kindly says good-bye.

In the room we just look at each other. We can't speak. Everybody's eyes are filled with tears. But nobody dares to show it.

What now? Everybody can go wherever they want when they are healthy. Now we are free. We are no longer under the Germans.

Later, Marco comes back and asks if we want to go to Palestine. He can register the three of us as Palestinian or as British citizens. He tells us that Munkacs will be under the Russians. And once that happens, we will not be able to leave.

We ask for some time to think about it. After a few hours, we decide to stay with our initial feeling: we are going home. We are going home to look around our town. And after that we will emigrate somewhere. Marco agrees with our plan, although he fears it might then be too late to get out. But he doesn't want to argue with us. In a case like this, you can't tell someone what to do. So we will be registered as Munkacsi and as Hungarians.

We talk about the past and the future. And about the future and the past. We have suffered enough. Now good will come. Let the sunshine brighten our life.

As far as food is concerned, it's not even news anymore. I think we could get back very fast to a regular life—a normal, human way of life, as we were used to years before.

I was liberated in a prisoner-of-war camp among very fine people. They took care of us with goodwill and compassion. Life is unusual. And so is this liberation. Who knows where my poor father is suffering? Who knows what he is thinking about his family among whom hardly anyone remains? Who knows where he is liberated? Who knows where and when I will see him again?

Father, you are alone, and you are my only thought. I am liberated, but I am afraid to go home. I am afraid what I will find, what I will not find. But let's wait now. We shall see what will happen. Let there be peace. Peace of mind.

AS IT COMES

Floating

W HEN I WROTE in my diary in the hospital, I did not know if my father had survived. I sensed, somehow, that he had; but I had no way of being certain. That would take three more months, when I finally was ready to leave the hospital and go home. Still, in a way that is hard to explain today, I could live with that uncertainty. Indeed, living without planning ahead, living from moment to moment, had become our habit. Within the camps, only the new arrivals and the fortune tellers believed in the future. For the rest of us, the terror and the immediate struggle to survive were all the calendar we had.

In a different way, a much more pleasant way, many of us also lived day by day in the first months after the liberation. Although I was ill—I had been diagnosed with tuberculosis—I remember these months in the hospital as a carefree time out of time, one of the nicest periods of my life. Living from minute to minute, we appreciated any small thing that happened—a meal, a laugh, a game, a story, a conversation with Marco or one of the others. Surrounded by the camaraderie of all, we let ourselves sink into the rediscovered comforts of simply living, without plans or tasks beyond our own recuperation. One thing led to another, and most of it was good. Without a time like that, simply floating on the current, savoring friendship and belonging, I doubt that I could have returned to life at all.

Journey's Beginning

IN EARLY AUGUST 1945, three months after the liberation, I was ready to go home. Or, to say it more truthfully, I knew the time had come. My physical strength had largely returned. The former POW camp was breaking up—every day our friends were departing for their own homes. Day by day, this shelter into which I had retreated was coming undone.

I remember the pain of the last day. Marco was even more attentive than usual. Somehow he had managed to get a horse and buggy for us, and this would be our transportation to Prague, the first stop on the journey home. He made sure I would be sheltered from the sun. We talked about staying in touch and meeting again in Palestine. Both of those things came true, although the second came at a much later date than I then had hoped. The thought of going out into the world scared me. And the thought of once again leaving the person on whom I most relied, even if not forever, was almost impossible to bear. This may have been the last time in my life that I cried. It may have also been the last time that I let myself feel like a child, which, at sixteen years old, I still was. But once the carriage started to move, I was numb.

The journey had begun.

The Capital of the Displaced

In the summer of 1945, Prague was a chaos of searching. It seemed that half of Europe was on the road, looking for the other half who were looking in turn. With everyone searching, the world was ripe with rumors and near-misses. "I know you from home!" "No, it's someone else." "I saw him on a train." "He left just yesterday." "They may be coming back tomorrow." "They may not be coming back at all."

Prague was a collection point, one of the capitals of the displaced. People registered there, posted notices and representatives, followed whatever leads toward finding someone, toward *having* someone. In Prague, people lived through their eyes, looking for some someone who might appear at any time.

Often enough, in ways both expected and completely unanticipated, someone did appear. Marika and her sister found an aunt who had been in Theresienstadt and, like us, also in Ravensbruck. The sisters knew that both of their parents were gone. Having found this much of their family, they stayed on in Prague.

Someone also found me. At one of the information centers, a man asked me, "Where are you from? What is your name?" When I told him, he said, "What are you doing here? Your father is home!" This was the first definite word; the man was from our area and seemed to be certain. Still, I knew that Prague was a city of wishes. Afraid of disappointment, I did not let myself fully believe him. I would have to see for myself.

Royal Welcomes

It took ten days to get the train that would bring me closer to home. The cars were packed with Russian soldiers, and the trains seemed to carry as many people hanging on to the outside as were jammed inside. It was not obvious which were the better berths.

We stopped in Bratislava and then, finally, Budapest. I went to the building, a school, where we searcher-survivors registered—the familiar boards of messages and lists. A short man stood in front of the lists, reading the names from the bottom up (I don't know why this detail always comes back to me). I recognized him—a cousin of mine. Wanting it to be a surprise,

I came up behind him and said, as casually as I could, "Are you looking for someone?"

He turned around and almost passed out. "I'm looking for you!" My father had heard I was coming, and he was afraid to leave Munkacs in case I arrived while he was gone. So he had his own searchers looking, whoever was traveling and could scan the lists.

My cousin went on to Prague, but he asked a friend of his who had been in the Czech army to help me get the train from Budapest to Munkacs. Things were looking up. This train was less crowded. And, for part of the way, I had my own military escort.

To say it differently, I was still sixteen and appearances mattered. Despite everything, and also because of everything, I was determined to return in style. I wore spike heels, a nice sweater, a white sailor-style outfit, and carried a shoulder bag. I decided that was elegant enough, but, as a final touch, I took the fiacre, a horse-drawn taxi, from the station in Munkacs to the house where I had learned my father was staying.

My cousin, Eva, was sitting in the window and saw me arrive. She called out, "Where have you been, you little stinker? Everybody else is home already!" I return from the war and this is my reception! In fact, they had been upset; most of the survivors were already back. They didn't know I had been ill or why it had taken me so long.

Still, I was not to be deterred. I marched into the house, put my bag down, and said: "This is very nice, but we're not going to stay here. It will soon be occupied by the Russians. So we should get ready to leave."

The world and Marco had taught me a lot. This was my first announcement.

Daughter

THE REUNION WITH my father was incredible, almost unreal.
To see each other again after all that had happened was the fulfillment of a dream. I was, indeed, not alone. We survived, not
only as two individuals, but as the remnants of a family. I was
one of the lucky ones, and I knew it.

Still, it is not surprising that I did not come back as the
daughter I had been. As my announcement conveyed (and was
meant to convey), I now had my own ideas about the practicali-
ties of life—where we could stay and where we must go—and
I wanted to be heard. For the most part, my father understood

this. It took a couple of months to convince him, but he eventually agreed that Munkacs could not be our future. Just before they closed the border, in November, we left.

I also came back with my own values. Reinforced by my conversations with Marco, I had become a committed Zionist. My goal was to help build a new Jewish homeland in Israel, along with Marco and so many others. This dream was not to come true for me, and it took a long time to accept that—not fully until we were already in America—as I will describe.

My father and I did not talk about all that had happened during the time we had been apart, and particularly not the terrible year from April to April, 1944–45. I think he was afraid to know, and perhaps we were each afraid to face it in the look, in the eyes, of the other. My mother, my little brother, everything was gone. Does anyone come back a "daughter" after that?

Outsiders

I WAS BACK in Munkacs, but I now knew for certain that that was not the same as being home. My father had returned much earlier; he was one of the first ones liberated by the Soviets in October 1944, and he had rented a large house that had become the community center for the displaced in our area. Like the centers in Prague or Budapest, almost everyone coming back passed through our house, looking for others, staying for a meal or staying for a week, sometimes trying to get belongings out of their former homes, now occupied by others. My father and I never revisited our own house from before. Here again, there was no return.

Still, the mood was not one of grief, perhaps because there was simply too much to grieve. As I had experienced in the hospital, people lived for the day, for the moment, not worrying too much about the future and yet not quite believing in it either.

The main thing, once again, was to have someone. There were weddings every day. People would hear about one couple getting married and say to each other, "Why don't we get married too! The Gypsy musicians are already here, the wine is open, the food has arrived—why not?" And so they did. People got married in groups, in epidemics. Why not?

This was the life. "Oh, you're going to America? Me too! Me too!" People might not know precisely how or when, but almost everyone knew they were leaving, and that was a big part of our giddiness. On the outside we were happy—living for the wedding or the music or the next glass of wine. On the inside? I'm not sure there was an inside. We were outsiders through and through.

Belongings

For us, the first stop would be Košice in Czechoslovakia, the town we also knew by its Hungarian name, Kassa. My Aunt Margitka lived there, my mother's sister, and we would be staying with her. But we already knew that it was only a station along the way. My father had made contact with his own sister who had emigrated to the United States almost thirty years earlier. Philadelphia became our ultimate destination and, despite my dreams of Israel, it was clear that I would be going to America as well.

In any case, it was one step at a time. The first member of

our family to leave Munkacs was a horse. "Sharika" had been with my father since he had returned to town and was adored by everyone, treated more like a pet than a working animal. Knowing the difficulty of carrying even minimal property across the border—people's belongings were constantly being confiscated—my father had hired a Russian soldier who was willing to drive Sharika and a buggy full of whatever we had to Košice. One man, a friend of ours, begged us to include his gold watch as well, an heirloom that he was sure would have the safest crossing with Sharika and the Russian. As it turns out, only Sharika and the buggy made it to Košice. Our belongings, the gold watch, and, eventually, the Russian all disappeared along the way.

So things seemed to go. We eventually took a train from Munkacs to Košice, and I recall one woman who had wanted to bring something from her yard. She had a bundle of dried fruit— what we called *sushanka*—that she had picked from her own trees. She carried the treasure on her back, and every time someone walked by her on the train, in went a hand, and out went one more portion of *sushanka*. For her, too, only memories could be salvaged—of tastes and textures and tangible belonging.

The Lucky Ones

LIFE IS MADE through belonging, through deepening connections. For some, the lucky ones, belonging coincides with where they happen to find themselves, with what they call "home." For others, probably a lot more others than we usually imagine, home has to be recreated, improvised, again and again. Those who are able to recreate it—and it takes more than their own efforts alone—are also the lucky ones.

I was a lucky one again in Košice. My Aunt Margitka became the most precious person in my life, and, in important ways, she still is. She represented my mother in her care and in her principles. As in other relationships I have described, we adopted each other, recreating family and home. But with my aunt it was also different, because this was a real relationship, based on genuinely knowing each other. So here it was not only an assertion of care, as vital and stubborn as that could be. Here, it was the full and actual thing.

In Košice, I heard her story:

She had been imprisoned in Budapest because she claimed responsibility for an infraction in order to protect her husband. They thought the authorities would punish a woman less severely. Ill and nearly starved, she survived and returned to Košice in early 1945, shortly after the Russians had liberated Budapest. Her husband and their two children were gone; she did not know where. The caretaker of her home was still there, so she was able to find shelter in her own house.

Slowly, her strength returned. She became one of the searchers, looking for whomever in her family might still be alive. And she was sought in turn. One day a man came up to her on the street, calling affectionately, "My dear! My dear!" So gaunt had he become, that she did not recognize her husband.

Both their children had been killed in Auschwitz. She blamed herself, feeling that she should have been at home, that there would have been something she could have done. That guilt has stayed with her all these years. But so has her humor, her intelligence, and her incredible determination.

So here we were—a child in search of a mother and a mother in search of a child. It was a natural pairing, to be sure. But that is only a recipe. The meal itself is much more interesting.

Days and Nights

WITH MY AUNT'S help, we did create a family again in Košice. I was with my father, his brother, two aunts from my father's side and their husbands, including Goldie, whom I had seen that day in Birkenau, and my cousin Eva who had greeted me from the window. All of us lived together in the same house, and the atmosphere was light and fun. I made friends, went to parties, and played at being in school. We knew we would be leaving before long—in a year we would move again to Teplice-Šanov, near Prague, to wait for emigration papers—so Košice was another place where life could be lived on the surface most of the time, which was probably where we needed it to be.

I remember my uncle would tease me about my lack of education. He was in love with theater and music and opera, and so he took me to performances and taught me to waltz around the apartment. I loved books, which were also a passion of his. I used to read late into the night, and my aunt would come in to make me turn off the light. She wanted me to get some sleep. Actually, she didn't just turn off the light, she removed it from the room. I would go to my uncle with a formal request: "Sir, would you be good enough to arrange a return of my light?" And he did!

Night was also the time when it was harder to stay on the outside and on the surface. Sleep brought dreams; dreams brought nightmares and memories. As I described, when I was in Auschwitz I dreamed of warmth and security, of being in my mother's lap. Now that I was away from Auschwitz, and lived in the warmth and security of our surviving family, my dreams took me back to the horror and the flames.

In April 1946, one year after the liberation, I awoke from a nightmare and wrote about it. As I read the pages today, it is hard to recall all that I was feeling then. I remember the days from this period much more than the nights, which I suppose is always how it is. But my writing documents the other world I continued to visit and which continued to visit me. I even gave a title to my reflection, "Auschwitz: The Endless Haunting." At that time, "endless" meant one year.

April 1946. Auschwitz: The Endless Haunting

The sound on the radio tells me it's twelve o'clock. I'm sitting and I'm thinking back. The sound of the music tears at my heart because it always takes me back and makes me remember. Remember what? Don't ask. I shouldn't even write it. It's Auschwitz. Auschwitz and its flames and its electrified barbed wire.

I'm standing all alone in a large crowd. My face is close to the wires. I'm looking into the distance. I want to muffle the sounds that I hear, but they are too close. Just a little quiet, a little peace, a few people—that's all I want around me. Not even other people, but just myself alone. I'd like to be able to think, but thinking is impossible.

Beyond the wire fence there is another crowd of people. But these are different from ourselves. These people are free. They are the ones who rule over us. They are the Germans. God, suddenly I can't even find words to describe them properly.

God, You took my mother away, and my little brother. Where did You take them? To the fire?

I'm looking into the fire. And I think I would go completely crazy if I thought that You, God in Heaven, You are also looking upon all of this. And You have not gone crazy.

You looked upon us while the innocent children, and my dear ones, were taken there. To us You granted the gift of having to suffer, of having to see all of this, and of having to continue to exist. To the Germans, You gave Your mercy. They listened to the music in freedom. We were there to play the music for them. We played and we listened through our broken hearts. We were their prisoners. We were the ones whose minds You took away completely.

So I'm standing. And I'm gazing. And the music plays unceasingly in my ears. It takes me home, sometimes all the way back home.

Can anyone comprehend what is happening? Broken-hearted Jewish prisoners are playing romantic music, the music of broken hearts. They play "In Havana" and other sentimental pieces. They play "The Angels Are Singing When You Talk To Me, My Sweetheart." They are playing "Mama."

The others, the killers, the ruthless German guards with their wine bottles, with their cigarettes, are enjoying themselves. They are having a party. If we are lucky, they will throw down a cigarette butt. One of us will pick it up.

We are their prisoners, doomed to death. And I can only call us stupid, ignorant, crazy. Because to live like this—denied everyone and everything, kicked and shoved underfoot, degraded and humiliated, doped and numb—only people who would just as soon be dead could live through this. Having lived it, we are no longer among the living. The living could not survive it.

Now, suddenly, I realize I have tears in my eyes. They are streaming down my face. Suddenly, I feel like I am home again, with my family. I am with those who were everything to me. It feels like so long, long ago, that we were all together.

But the fire, the cursed flames, still don't let me think. They wake me up from my dreams, and my dreams hold the only hope for going on. The flames have awakened me again. Their hissing and crackling have awakened me again.

God, Oh God, give me a little strength. Give me a little sense, and take away the daze. I would like to be able to think that it still might be true that somebody, somewhere, waits for me.

This cannot be true. That I am here, on this earth, all by myself. That there is fire. That there are people. That there are bones. That there are the suffocated innocents. This is impossible. That ours, that mine, are there.

So perhaps it is good that I can only think rarely. And rarely do I come to my senses. For it seems like now, at these moments, I am out of the daze. I can think clearly. I can see the whole truth.

You can do without mind and thought and still exist. But a living human being has to think. Therefore, we are not human beings anymore. We can't call ourselves human because we can no longer think. And without this, life ceases to be life. It is gone completely.

I feel like a dead, degraded, cowardly Jew. And tomorrow, maybe tonight, I will have to get up to work and put on a living face. I will have to sew up the clothes and cut up the material left by those who have gone to the flames. I will have to listen to the humiliating curses and feel completely numb and ignorant. All of this is true. All of this is real.

My thoughts have started to wander again. They are wandering to Auschwitz. They are visiting the flames. They are in Heaven and talking with God. And who knows where else they are wandering?

My pen wants to go on and on, by itself. It is sliding from my hand. At times like this my strength leaves me. It leaves me each time I see it all again. It leaves me when I see the truth once more.

Music is supposed to be a good tonic. It's supposed to quiet your nerves. And so it quiets mine. But now I am turning off the radio. I don't want music. I don't want Auschwitz music. I don't want flame music. I don't want to see it all again. I don't want the haunting.

Now I ask You, God, again:

Give me a little, peaceful dream. Or no dream at all. Because yesterday and always I only dream about my dead ones. This is not true, God! Tell me it's not true! And tell me I'm not questioning You in such an ugly way.

Now, as a cowardly soul, I beg Your forgiveness. I thank You for at least giving my father back to me. Please give him peace of mind in his life. Give peace and well-being to all my loved ones. Give me no more dreams that will make me think back and remember again. Give me quietness.

God in Heaven, Amen.

Contradictions

We survivors are bundles of contradictions. We argue with God, and the next moment we ask for His forgiveness. We push away the past, and we are constantly drawn back to it. When we are here, we are also there. And when we are there, we are also here. A sound, a smell, a feeling may be all it takes to bring it back. And even the past is split in two—memories of home, which we usually try to recapture; and memories of the destruction of home, which we usually try to forget.

So there are many strands at once. One world reminds us of the other; one thought leads to the next, and into the past. That is the reason, probably not the usual reason, that we never feel whole. It is not that our joys are not real. They are entirely real. It is just that they never exist simply by themselves. They are always in reference to something else, something that can consume them in an instant. And then there are simply the blank spaces. The spaces where things were that are not anymore. Even when home and life are recreated, the losses are never made whole.

Many years after the war, after I had arrived in Michigan where I live now, I used to visit a tree that grew in our neighborhood. Actually, it didn't grow anymore because it had died years before, and they never cut it down. But the shape was still there, the branches, the curves—it was still beautiful. I looked forward to driving down that street.

Perhaps it reminded me of the tree in Munkacs where Marika and I used to meet and solve the problems of our world. Perhaps it stood for our world itself, or ourselves. But I don't want to make it too complicated. A month after I wrote "The Haunting Horror," I wrote another reflection about my feelings. It is shorter and simpler.

May 6, 1946

God, what's wrong with me? I'm choked with my own cry. I would like to cry, but I can't. Today, too, I came home full of anger. For no reason. I went to the theater and to a coffeehouse. And my poor companion couldn't figure out what happened to me, to this unfortunate crazy soul. He couldn't understand my behavior. He questioned me, but unsuccessfully. I couldn't answer it. I could find no reason myself. How could I answer it? One thing I can say: To think back is very painful. And I'm longing after a mother.

Murcos

There are some stories about longing and belonging that tell themselves:

My aunt and uncle owned a moving company in Košice, and Murcos drove the horse and wagon that they used to deliver coal and other goods. "Murcos," I am sure, was not his given name—it means "gruff" or "angry" in Hungarian, and, on the surface, that's what he always was. He was also almost always drunk. Indeed, the horse knew the way to the bar and could deliver him there on its own.

Murcos had worked for my aunt for many years, long before

she was married or had a family. They had an amazing relationship—constantly arguing, particularly about his drinking, but also gently teasing and warm. She used to say that she had to get Murcos's approval before she married her husband, and Murcos was not forthcoming. "Such a *skinny* one you had to pick? That was the only one you could find?"

During the months I spent in Košice, Murcos and I also became close. And when I finally left to join the family in Teplice-Šanov, he cried bitterly. He asked if I would leave him a photo, to kiss every time he went to the bar. My aunt later told me that, after I left, he was drunk for a week, crying and holding the picture.

A couple of years later, my aunt and uncle left Košice for good. They were going to Israel. Shortly after they departed, Murcos was found dead in a ditch. There was no one there to care for him. He had no one for whom to care.

Arriving and Departing

IN 1947 WE moved to Teplice-Šanov in order to be near Prague and to be ready, when our papers came through, to go to the States. By now I had almost accepted the destination, because this was where my family was going and the affidavits from my aunt in Philadelphia were already on the way. If my Košice aunt and uncle had already been in Israel, it may have been different, but that was still a couple of years away. In any case, I was told that if I was still not happy in America, I could leave from there. Arriving and departing had become a way of life, so it seemed a plausible choice.

Teplice-Šanov was another year of days and nights—enjoy-able, carefree activities during most of my time awake; and nightmares every night. In this, I was like many others. Most of us who had been in the camps or lived similar horrors had nightmares, and we took them for granted. There was more than one world in this world. In Europe so soon after the war, nobody doubted that. Even when the nightmares were at their worst, when it could take several people to wake me up and bring me back, it did not seem like a long journey from one landscape to the other. Here, too, arriving and departing had become a way of life.

Working Girls

As departing from Czechoslovakia drew nearer, we wondered what we would be able to bring with us. The border was tightly controlled, and people were allowed to take out very little. But small "gifts" to the customs officers were also traditional, and they could help increase one's allowance.

So my father and I tried it. But, as they searched through our bags, not simply removing things but throwing them out the window, we realized we had miscalculated. Thinking the officers would be more lenient with a young person, particularly a girl (I had learned from my aunt), I immediately confessed that I had packed the offending items. I was not familiar with all the regulations. It didn't work. They tore up several of our papers and threw both my father and me in jail.

To be truthful, jail was not all bad. My father and I talked with each other through the window when the men took exercise in the courtyard. I wondered if this might mean that I wouldn't be going to America after all. And, indeed, my father said that, when we got out of there, perhaps we would end up going to Palestine.

Still, in the beginning, I was distressed. The rest of the family had left for Sweden from where the ship would be departing, and here were my father and I, locked up and left behind. There were several other young women, really girls, in my cell; but I felt very much alone.

As I cried, I heard one of the girls say, "Hey, she's not one of us, is she? Which corner was yours?"

"Corner? What?"

I heard them talk among themselves. "Who is she? What is she doing here?"

They came over, and I told them my story. I then started to cry again, and they took me under their wing. They protected me like a little sister, and suddenly, even among the working girls, I had found another small family.

In fact, we were, in a sense, related. They told me about their *maly tlusty*—a roly-poly little man—who was their favorite, the doctor who took care of them. It turns out that the little *maly tlusty* was my cousin, then head of the venereal diseases department at the main hospital in Teplice-Šanov. Once they knew I was their doctor's cousin, I was declared family forever.

Here also, then, was a bit of an education—jail is jail, but this incarceration was infinitely sweeter than the ones I had known before. When my father and I were finally released one month later, my new friends and I said good-bye with genuine sadness. And then I did the two things I had dreamed about behind bars: I took a bath and went to the beauty parlor.

It also turned out we were not too late to get the ship. There would be no last-minute chance to go to Israel. It was north to Sweden, and on to one more chapter of this life.

Gripsholm

THE CROSSING WENT well, at least for me—I was the only one in the family who didn't get seasick. But all of us found the *Gripsholm* to be an agreeable ship—not that we had many other ocean voyages for comparison—and we were eager to get to America.

By now I really had accepted that this was the next step. One night, on board the ship, I had a dream in which I actually said aloud, "You have to take life as it comes." My cousin was sleeping in the same cabin. "What did you say?" she asked. "You have to take life as it comes," I repeated, still asleep. She told me about it the next day. "You said, 'You have to take life as it comes.'"

And so the small, mostly seasick, group of us prepared to take life as it came—as new experiences came, and as memories came, too.

AMERICA

Slow Boat To China

STRANGELY ENOUGH, ONE of my first impressions of America was a song lyric. I remember, almost at the same moment we landed, hearing the line, "I'm going to get you on a slow boat to China." And I thought to myself, "I just got off the boat from Sweden, and they're sending me out already!"

But the welcome was warm. My aunt was waiting for us when we docked. Everyone cried—the joy of the arrival, the reunion, and perhaps also being done with the rolling sea. The customs process went quickly; our papers were in order, and we were soon on our way.

My aunt had brought two cars in order to accommodate all of the uncles, aunts, and cousins. Before we drove back to Philadelphia, we all went out for lunch at a dairy restaurant in New York. For one of my uncles, whom everyone thought resembled the Hungarian character actor Szoke Szakal because of his pronounced double chin, this was pure ecstasy. He loved dairy food, and he could hardly believe the treasures that were spread before us—cheeses, blintzes, bowls of sour cream! "You mean I can have all the sour cream that I want?! Just pick it up with the spoon! We didn't have this in Czechoslovakia."

We had arrived in the Promised Land. There was no doubt about the milk; perhaps the honey would be next.

Ei-yocks

Actually, the toilet was next. This was not because American plumbing was, in some essential way, different from what we were used to. Rather, it was a problem of translation. The first day, arriving at my aunt's house, my father asked where he should hang up his coat. "In the closet," said my aunt. "The closet?" To us, "closet" meant "water closet," and storing something for safekeeping was the last thing one would want to do there. "So this is how my sister greets me!" my father exclaimed. "I haven't seen her for thirty-five years, and she wants me to hang my coat in the closet!?"

Language was our battle in those years. Understanding and being understood—even about small things—was a perpetual challenge. This was true in spite of some of the most sincere efforts. One of the American boys I dated came from a Hungarian Jewish family, and he was proud of the fact that he could speak a few words. He was trying his best both to impress me and help me feel at home. We had gone to an amusement park together, and he asked if I would like a *forro kutya*. *Forro* means "hot." *Kutya* means "dog." I jumped. "Just because I come from Europe, you think we eat dogs?" As you hear, we were a sensitive group.

My uncle Mano found his Waterloo when my aunt sent him to the store to buy some Ei-yocks. "Can you direct me to the Ei-yocks?" he asked the clerk.

"What?"

"Ei-yocks."

"Eggs?"

"No."

"Hocks?"

"No."

"No?"

"No. *Ei-yocks.*"

"We don't have any *ei-yocks*."

"No Ei-yocks?"

"*No ei-yocks.* We have got *no* ei-yocks in the store."

"They have got no Ei-yocks in the store," my uncle announced when he returned. "Of course they do," my aunt insisted, "Bring the can." She handed him the container of *Ajax.*

My uncle went back to the store. Armed with the can, he brought it to the skeptical clerk.

"Ei-yocks!" he exclaimed. "For cleaning the closet."

Private Lives

LIKE ALL OF us, Uncle Mano lived more than one life. Music, particularly orchestral music, was his greatest passion. He had all the phonograph records and would stand at the center of the room, conducting. He knew these pieces inside and out, and so he really *was* conducting, cuing each section and even individual musicians. He lived every note coming and going, in joyous anticipation and in loving memory. He did not have the money to go to an actual concert, so he invited the orchestra into his bustling imagination. Listening to him, just watching him, was my own musical education.

I shared a room with my American cousin, and, in general, we got along well. She used to read the movie magazines, and I devoured books, not understanding half of what I read, but doing what I could to learn the language. Sometimes hand signs were more useful in any case. When my cousin had a blind date, I stationed myself at the bottom of the stairs and signaled up whether this one called for high or low-heeled shoes.

Looking back, I would describe this as a happy time—there were family gatherings, parties, and dates like my friend with the *forro kutya*. Still, my diary tells another side. I was frustrated by not being able, and certainly not being encouraged, to go to school, which was what I had really wanted to do. At twenty years old, and after all the moves and changes, I was worried that my life was going in no perceptible direction—very much like the self-questioning of a lot of twenty-year-olds, although no one talked about that at the time.

Even within my family, I was feeling increasingly separated. My aunt treated me with kindness, but I was not her own daughter, and she had clearly different expectations about the education I required, the interests I should pursue, and the money I ought to spend—even if it was money I had earned myself. My father and I were still very close, but there was also a strain in our relationship. When we were still in Czechoslovakia, he remarried. He had asked my permission, which was a sign of how much we were no longer father and daughter in the old-fashioned way. Of course, I gave it and I was happy for him. But his new wife and I did not always have an easy relationship. At the end of 1949 they moved from Philadelphia to Detroit, so in that way, too, I was on my own again.

It is impossible to separate these personal strands from the wider mood of America in the 1950s. Certainly this was not, in general, a time for soul-searching and reflection. The war was over, the soldiers were home, it was time to move onward and forward. If one had memories, they were one's own responsibility; if one had nightmares, that was one's own business. And so, when memories came, and memories came every day and certainly every night, they came to me privately and alone. That, above all, is the story that my diary from this period retells. I was writing on the fifth anniversary of the liberation, and, on this day at least, those years seemed long indeed.

April 1950 – Philadelphia

Five years is like half a century when you live your life with bitterness and reminiscing. Even when you are at a party, and you are in a good mood, later you realize your guilt. Is this anger? Is this conscience? Is this self-awareness or self-criticism?

But why? This is a mystery deep within the soul. And what do you want, my soul, if I can call you that? Five years—it doesn't take long to write it down, and it's easy to say it. But when I remember, I am carried back even more clearly than anytime before. But why?

It's five years today that I was liberated from the Germans' chain. In my egotistic human way, I was happy then that I existed, that I remained alive. I was happy for every given day and for every bite that I received. But I didn't live yet, I just thought I lived. My head was full of haze. I didn't plan because I thought everything came naturally, by itself. To like and be liked I took for granted, and I didn't know that I would always and always be carried back.

I had just stepped into life's school. I was only a child then, but the dolls with which I used to play were far from me. I had to mature very quickly, but it was too fast and it didn't bring any fruit. Because, at this stage of my life, I still can't give myself any clear ideas.

I don't know what I am, and I don't know when I'm doing right or wrong. Am I right when I am thinking? And for *what* I am thinking? Many times, I think I was just born for trouble. And to be a burden and sorrow to everybody, because I cannot laugh. They say, "If you laugh, everybody laughs with you, and if you cry, you cry alone."

Yes, my diary, here I am—in America! After many fights I consented to come here to be with my family rather than go to Palestine. I didn't take things as seriously then, which is why I'm fighting now. Every day is a fight, because I'm trying to make myself understood.

My rights, my principles, and somebody else's—with my own double standards!

But nobody's right and nobody's wrong. Only the truth is right, but that is so rare. Now I'm pushing the years back. For me, that's like putting the clock back a few minutes. Time elapses, but the impossible does not fade from my eyes.

Five years ago I finished my diary with a sentence that was full of hope that I will see my father again. Yes, God helped me, and my dream became a reality. We met in my hometown and with unbelievable happiness we were reunited. But my father left our home when I was a child, when he was taken away to a forced labor camp. Later he discovered that his daughter had her own thoughts about life's problems.

I knew we should get out of my hometown because it would be Russian. And I also knew that in my hometown, where I lived my sweetest, happiest time, that life would never return. I wanted to escape from the memories because I didn't want to live through, first the good, then the miserable destroying of life.

Either way, for us to pack and leave meant little. We'd already tasted wandering, and it seems like this is the pattern of our lives—pack and go; pack and go.

Soul-Searching

LOOKING BACK AT what I wrote in Philadelphia that day, I am surprised by some of the distress I expressed. Although I remember writing those lines, I have a hard time remembering the writer. Was I really that angry? Did I fight outwardly or only inwardly? Was I truly unable to laugh?

I mainly recall the inner struggle. I judged, and then I judged myself for judging. I did laugh—I remember many good times with friends and family—but it did not seem to be enough: not happy-go-lucky, American, lighthearted enough. Of course, that was because it wasn't. I blamed myself for taking life too seriously and then for not taking it seriously enough. In another entry, I wrote just a single line: "It's hard to be smart; but it's harder yet, with a smart head, to live as though ignorant."

The core was always the pull of the memories themselves. I wrote that I was carried back "even more clearly" than before. I felt that these memories and the truths they contained demanded something of me, but I was not sure what. Unlike immediately after liberation, it was not enough to live day by day simply being grateful to have survived. I wanted to *do* something with my life. In Israel, building a new country, it would have been clear what that meant. But what did "doing something" mean in Philadelphia? And how was one to do it on one's own?

Greeners

F OR MOST OF us, during these years, doing something meant learning the language, establishing ourselves in whatever way we could, starting families. We did not forget what we had experienced, but we generally kept it to ourselves. It was the practical things that mattered, and soul-searching was for diaries and personal letters and, often enough, late-night conversations between us when, whether we intended it or not, we found ourselves back among the memories. We did, indeed, learn to "cry alone." If we sometimes protested, those protests were almost always private as well—again, topics for the diary or for late-night thoughts.

Like other immigrants before us, we were the "green-horns"—the "greeners" as they said—with all the condescension that implied. Also like other immigrant groups, we tended to create a community together—a reflection of our shared distance from the mainstream and our shared struggles with language and getting established. Those of us who did not go to regular school often found ourselves together in night school or in similar jobs. And, of course, we shared memories, not only of the destruction but of the life before.

In 1950, I moved from Philadelphia to Detroit, in part to be closer to my father. A good number of survivors had come to Detroit to work in the automobile industry, and the community was particularly well developed. Many of us lived in the same neighborhood around Dexter Boulevard. Zukin's was the local ice cream parlor where everybody congregated and where it was always easy to meet friends. There was a promenade for evening walks and socializing.

Compared with Philadelphia, I loved this new environment and its bustling social life. If I still didn't know what I was trying to accomplish, I was certainly less alone. When we went to the movies, one would tell the other who told the others until, soon enough, it was one big group. "What's playing? Let's go! Let's go!" There were soccer games every week that everyone attended until most of the boys got married. That was the end of the soccer games because almost no one could afford medical insurance, and soccer was too dangerous a pastime for a man with real responsibilities!

And so we made our strangely hybrid, somewhat separated, nightly haunted, American lives. We laughed and discovered that—notwithstanding its promise—the "whole world" was *not* "laughing with us." They were otherwise engaged. But the important thing was that it was real laughter all the same.

Both Right

I was with another date when I met Zoli at a party. Later, he told me that a friend of his had pointed me out and said, "That's the girl for you." "No, not that one," he had apparently replied, "She's too stuck up."

And, of course, I thought Zoli was pretty stuck up himself. He asked for my telephone number, and I said that I did not give out my number for the little black book. If he wanted to call, my father was listed in the directory. He could reach me there.

As far as being stuck up, we were probably both right.

A few days after the party, we accidentally met again in

front of Hudson's in downtown Detroit. We talked for a few minutes and before we parted, he said, "You know, you are going to be my wife."

"Well then, *mazel tov* to us!" I replied.

As far as being stuck up, we were probably both right.

Our Place

*M*AZEL *TOV.* ZOLI and I got married in August of 1951 in Philadelphia. My whole family gathered, and the reception was in a catering restaurant that my aunt owned. Zoli was, as he said, the only stranger at the wedding. He had no surviving relatives in the U.S. except for one distant cousin who served as best man. And, of course, we had each other.

We also had our home in Detroit, an apartment we rented that was our pride and joy. It was on the ground floor, which meant that, if you wanted, you could go in and out through the window—one of its charming and practical features. It also had a Murphy bed that had to be tied up to the couch to keep it from jumping, uninvited, out of the wall. And it had green, horribly dark green, wallpaper. Soon after we moved in, my cousin came over to take a look. She came in. And she kept looking at the walls. And walking around. And staring at the walls. And saying nothing at all. And I was proud as I could be. Yes, it was ugly. It was dirty. But it was ours.

We gave it a complete makeover. We rented a sanding machine that we could get over the weekend at a better rate; and we attacked it inch by inch: sanding, scraping, cleaning, painting. Before long it was sparkling and beautiful. Even my cousin came back a few weeks later to see, as she said, what we had done with the dungeon. Now she was impressed! I recall one day we had just put up the new drapes. These were the icing on the cake, the final touch. After they were up, we went out into the hallway to take in the whole, magnificent scene. And down came the drapes! It didn't matter. It gave us a chance to put them up again.

But the best part was the company. People were always dropping by—in the door, through the window, whatever was most convenient. At any hour of the day or night, they just showed up. "What's cookin'?" announced one of our friends who knew the American idiom. "Hamburgers," I answered, looking at the stove. "And potatoes." I did not know the lingo. "Hamburgers are good," he responded. "Hamburgers are good."

There was no shortage. My father had a butcher shop, and he used to surprise us with meat. There was one package after the other, each carefully labeled with the date and the cut. We bought a freezer, but the only place there was room for it was in the bedroom. That was where it went. I draped it over so that it looked like a dresser.

So there we were—friends coming in the window and steak in the bedroom. It was a good life.

French Salad

ONE OF MY friends from these first years in Detroit deserves a chapter of her own. Indeed, she *was* a chapter of her own. I first met Cilike when Zoli and I were still dating. For several years, she and her husband were among our closest friends. We had dinner together almost every Sunday night.

Cilike drank, smoked, and swore like a sailor. Actually, like several sailors; actually, like a small ship. On her, it was charming. She was an artist, by craft and by soul, and everything she touched was transformed. So was everyone. Men were attracted to her. Stray dogs found their way to her. Anything that moved seemed to move her way.

For me, she was a mentor. Before Zoli and I got married, she insisted that we do so. "What are you waiting for? Do it!" She took me on as her student and insisted on showing me the ropes. "This is where to shop. This is what to cook. For this, you need to have a special knife. For that, you have to use a wooden spoon. Are you listening to me? This is important!" Of course, she said it more colorfully.

One day she invited me over for a special lunch. We were going to have "French salad," she announced. I didn't know what a "French salad" was, but she suggested it would not be our usual salami on rye bread with plenty of mayonnaise. In fact, the salad was full of things, including our beloved salami, but I am not sure to this day why it was "French." Cilike's declaration was enough to make it so.

She said there was something she had to tell me, and she was going to turn around before she did. She didn't want to see my reaction, or perhaps she wanted me to feel free to have whatever reaction I did. With her back to me, she said, "I have to tell you that I have been keeping a secret from you. I have to tell you that I am not Jewish."

There was a brief moment of silence. She turned to face me. "So what else is new?" I said. In fact, it was no secret. Other friends of ours had mentioned it. It had never made any difference, although we knew it had caused some strain with her husband's family. In any case, to Cilike, the declaration was important. The air had to be clear. Things had to be what they were. The salad was French. Cilike wasn't Jewish. Our lunch was as wonderful as always.

Years later she developed a very serious cancer. Late in the illness she called me and said she wanted us to go on one last trip together—to Las Vegas, one of her favorite places. As always, she drank, she smoked, she swore, and she had the time of her life. I remember the particular joy she got from the slot machines. She said she loved the sounds they made—the coins going in, the spinning drums, and, every now and then, the coins coming out. It wasn't the sound of money. It was the sound of daring, of chance. It was the echo of the long shot, while death was closing in.

Even Cilike couldn't conjure so large a jackpot. In my kitchen, where I'm always reminded of her, I keep a cookie jar that she gave me and that I now use as a planter. Everything that grows in there comes out lush and wild and beautiful. Needless to say.

Two Doors

We stayed in our beloved first apartment for five years and probably would have stayed longer if the rent had not gone up. Zoli had promised that for our fifth anniversary we would go to Europe. I said, either we take that trip or we buy a house. We bought the house.

In truth, it was a house-buying time, and many of our friends were also looking. Sunday was the outing day, and we would discuss the search together.

"Oh, did we see a house yesterday in Oak Park! It had two front doors! One house, and two front doors!"

He meant French doors, a sign of real grandeur. And someone said, "Why are you looking at a house with two doors? You
know you're not going to buy it!"

"Who knows? We might. We might. Then we have one for
coming in and one for going out."

People always say survivors are obsessed with food, and not
wasting any. Perhaps we are. But we are equally obsessed with
doors and paint and putting up drapes. Why? Because a house
becomes a home. And a home becomes a family. And starting all
over, in a new country, in a new life, that is almost everything.

Of course, there were hard times. I had warned Zoli before we
were married that I sometimes screamed during the night, from
nightmares. When I did scream, he would comfort me and talk
with me. Not necessarily about the nightmare but about the good
things in our lives, and the home we were making together. This
always brought me back, and the nightmares came less often.

So it seemed that the house of memory also had two doors—
one for going in and one for coming out.

The Hope Room

CHILDREN. AFTER WHAT we had seen, after everyone and everything we had lost, they were inevitably at the center. In our new house there was a "hope room," and there wasn't any question about what we were hoping for.

Our hopes were fulfilled: Vicki was born in 1959, Amy in 1960, Randy in 1964.

My precious aunt takes credit for Vicki, and she is probably right. I learned I was pregnant right after the first time she visited from Israel, and I have no doubt that the two are related. My aunt's presence always brought a special sense of security and well-being. She was my mother's representative, as she continues to be, and it was her nurture, I think, that prepared me to become a mother myself. While she was with us, I felt especially relaxed.

My aunt herself put it slightly differently and in the form of a somewhat risqué Hungarian expression. "I was holding the candle," she claimed.

The truth is that having children is never what a couple does all by themselves, and perhaps that is true in a particular way for survivors. Children represent whole families, even whole communities, extending themselves into the future. And so having children involves many more people than the parents and the children themselves. They are all, in a way, "holding the candle."

My aunt's second visit was scheduled to coincide with Amy's birth, but Amy surprised us and arrived a few weeks early. I remember how excited I was that my aunt was coming. It was a Friday night, and everything was laid out perfectly for Shabbat. The babies, the meal, the beautiful spring evening—the table was set for her visit. But the flight was late, Zoli took a wrong turn, the babies started crying, I was struggling to keep everything and everyone fresh and ready. It was a lost cause. By the time my aunt and Zoli got to the door, it was utter chaos.

It didn't matter. She stayed six months, and those months remain some of the fondest we remember. Having lost her own two children, my aunt relived her motherhood through my children, and especially through Amy, who needed, as a "preemie," special care.

My aunt went to work. She held her, rocked her, fed her,

fattened her, comforted her, and barely let me touch her. I remember waking up in the morning, surprised to have had a full night's sleep. "Oh, Margitka," I said to my aunt, "Isn't it nice that the baby slept through the night!" And she would say, "Yeah, it's wonderful." And meanwhile we could see how tired she was. But she never let on, and we never did either, that she was up much of the night, rocking and comforting Amy. The only cost was the separation when my aunt finally did have to return to Israel. It was a terribly painful farewell for all of us. But, this time, we knew there would also be a return.

My father also visited during this period. He and his wife were living in Los Angeles by this time, and if he didn't stay as long, he was equally attentive. One scene I will remember as long as I live. I was giving Amy a bath. And the two grandparents, my aunt and my father, were also participating. One held her tiny hand; one stroked her head. They were entirely involved. "Did you wash her finger?" "Did you wash her foot?" I see the focus in their eyes. The care. The awe. The absolute importance of this moment, of being together, of bathing this baby, of this little hand, of this little toe.

The Assembly Line

$\overline{\hspace{10cm}}$

PARTIES, HOLIDAYS, FAMILY gatherings. They are all celebrations of being together; affirmations of the fact that we are here.

My aunt and uncle who lived in Philadelphia never traveled. It was extremely difficult for them, but they decided to come to Randy's brit. I remember they carried a shoe box filled to the brim with homemade cookies and cakes. I recall that shoe box, the effort that it took to get to Detroit, how much they wanted to be there. It was the only time they visited, but the shoe box has stayed with us.

Vicki's bat mitzvah in 1972 was perhaps the most memorable gathering of all. Most of the family was still alive, and people came from everywhere. The Philadelphia cousins, my father from Los Angeles, friends from every corner. The reception was in our home, and everyone was involved. It was like Amy's bath on a larger scale—an assembly line that stretched from the kitchen, down the hallway, and into the laundry room where all the pieces were being put together.

One person was slicing the meat, another was putting it on the platter, the next was adding the greens. One dish at a time, made its way from the kitchen, down the hall, from hand to hand to hand.

Everyone was excited just to be part of it. We were laughing, joking, making up games and songs as we went along, recalling old ones. The preparation was more fun than the party. There was no difference between them.

Apart

BUT I AM leaving something out, a chapter between Randy's birth and Vicki's bat mitzvah that was one of the most painful in my life, even measured against the other painful times. Indeed, in some respects, this was the most difficult of all.

In the spring of 1966, a year and a half after Randy was born, the tuberculosis first diagnosed at liberation reemerged. I had to be hospitalized. Suddenly I was taken away from our young family—Zoli, our three children, all the day-to-day activities of our household. In those days, TB patients were quarantined in order to prevent exposing others to the infection. The length of quarantine was uncertain; it depended on the progress of the illness and, eventually, the evidence that it would yield to antibiotics that were still being developed. So I was entirely isolated from my family, and—to say it as I experienced it—I felt that I had lost my life, my world, all over again.

In some ways this was even worse than Auschwitz. Then I was a child. Now I had a family of my own for whom I was responsible and whose well-being was my purpose. And so I blamed myself for becoming ill. Along with the pain of separation was my guilt and frustration that I could not fulfill my tasks as a wife and mother. I was losing it all, and so were they.

In the beginning I fought it. I called home every few hours, trying to tell Zoli what the children should eat, what they should wear, how everything should be. But over the phone I'm hearing the crying, the commotion, and I had to realize that I couldn't control all of this long-distance. It was not possible. And so a part of me simply gave up. I had to let go.

Something similar happened with family visits. Zoli and the children could come to the hospital grounds, outside the ward, but I could not touch them or hold them for fear of spreading the infection. We could only look at each other from a distance, which was almost more painful than not seeing each other at all. A little later in the hospitalization, I was allowed to visit my home, but I was not allowed to stay overnight and, again, I could look at the children but not touch them.

This was the worst of all. Here I was, back in my home, surrounded by my family, and yet I was an outsider, a visitor from another planet. I remember one night, I was back at the house and, luckily for all of us, the children were asleep. From the distance of the door, I looked at each of them in their beds. I broke. I couldn't stand it. I said to Zoli, "Get me out of here! You get me out of here! I can't be back until I can really be back. I don't belong here anymore. This is terrible. This is torture."

Zoli argued, "No. You belong here. This is your home."

"No. Not now it isn't. Not right now it isn't."

I couldn't wait to get back to the hospital. The ward was where I belonged, and it made no sense to fight it. Perhaps someone else could have tolerated the frustration. But I was not that person, and I knew it.

It was also at this time that I turned again to my diary. I wrote about things that I have already recounted here about the deportation, arriving in Auschwitz, and my mother's final goodbye. This was the first time I wrote about them, in the tuberculosis ward at Henry Ford Hospital in 1966. Having again lost my world, I returned in reflection to 1944. The house of memory has two doors. One leads out. The other leads back in.

This was how I began:

The Hospital, 1966

After being established in the United States as a citizen, wife, and finally a mother of three young children, I was told that I was sick and would have to part from my family for an indefinite time of hospitalization. This agony evoked all the dormant horrors of being a camp inmate. As I entered the hospital corridor, it looked like a typical jail. I was becoming a prisoner all over again. Entering the room and meeting my roommate added to my sense of a nightmare returned. The lady was a German.

As a fifteen-year-old carefree child whose interests were school, family, and friends, I watched our little city of Munkacs become a strange place. It filled with Hungarian and German occupying soldiers. Our neighbors whom we'd known all our lives suddenly became alien to us. We had to wear the yellow star. Still, we walked our streets, not realizing the seriousness of the situation....

And so I retold the story of our gradual awareness of the real situation, of my father's departure, of our time in the brick factory, and, eventually, the cattle car. Now a mother myself, unable to care for my children, unable even to touch them, I remembered my own mother, her promise and her farewell, on the ramp at Auschwitz.

After three attempts to run back to the moving line, I was thrown to the sandy gravel, pleading with my mother. With a concerned ache in her eyes, she saw her child being thrown and pushed.

With a wave of her gentle hand, she accomplished what could not be done by bayonet. "Go, my child, go. We will see each other tomorrow."

The Ant Farm

As at Auschwitz, I gave up. At a certain point I did not fight the situation because it could not be changed. And yet, also as at Auschwitz, I did not give up. I could not control much, but there were still things that I could do. And, of course, for all the pain of separation, I knew that the ward was *not* Auschwitz. It was a place for healing and, in unexpected ways, a place for life.

My roommate, whom I represented in my diary as "a German," was, in fact, a kindly older woman. As it turned out, we got along well. We were there together, and, in this case, in very much the *same* world, not opposed ones.

And so, in fact, I was not alone. Many of us joined forces, and I will never forget our little group, from all backgrounds, who made a life together on that ward.

Earl had been a priest and was now a teacher. In a number of ways he became a teacher for many of us there. He was very knowledgeable, not only about Catholicism but about religion and philosophy in general. He and I had many talks about Christianity and Judaism, their similarities and their differences. We became good friends.

If Earl was our spiritual guide, I became a sort of physical therapist. I was encouraged by one of the nurses, an Irishwoman who was both our drill sergeant and our protector. On the outside, she was tough. I remember one of the other patients had a visitor once who complained, quite loudly, about having a headache that day. "Jesus, Mary, then what the hell are you coming here for then, and botherin' all of us?" our nurse proclaimed in full brogue. I am certain she scared the poor woman away.

I had started a walking program for myself, gradually building up from five minutes a day to ten minutes, and so on. Our nurse said to me, "Why don't you get all your guys out of their rooms? Take them off my hands and take them with you." And so I did. I knocked on doors. "Let's go for a walk." Little by little we had the whole group. We challenged each other, each drawing strength from the rest and from our group as a whole.

I will never forget Rosh Hashanah that fall. I had told some of the other patients about what I would have done at home—a house full of family and friends to celebrate the new Jewish year.

I had a small table in my hospital room where I lit the holiday candles. And everyone on the ward came by. They knocked on the door, brought a bit of food, and wished me a happy New Year. It was clear they really wanted to do this for me—their own little assembly line—and it was incredible.

And so we came to rely on each other. Even inside the hospital, our ward became a kind of haven. One elderly man was afraid of being sent to another floor; he wanted to stay with us. He had become very ill. In fact, he had terminal lung cancer, and that was why they wanted to move him to another part of the hospital. One evening he asked me to stay near him. Our nurse shooed me away—she wanted me to protect my own strength—but I stayed. He died that night. I was glad he did not die alone.

Bill had an ant farm in his room, one of those small squares of soil between two plates of glass through which you could see all of the ants' goings-on. I would visit him regularly to watch them—often enough that he eventually exclaimed, "Oh, it's you again! Are you here to visit me or the ants?"

In fact, we were both fascinated by them. "Look how they're working together! Look at the way they're carrying the food back and forth, making new tunnels, fixing the old ones." He had a whole book on the subject, and we followed the ants' progress as we, encased within the walls of a hospital ward, followed our own.

Who knows what worlds, what lives, may find their way on the margins, even in the barely conceivable space between two panes of glass?

Home

I CAME HOME from the hospital on Christmas Eve, 1966. I was cured of tuberculosis and that was wonderful. But it took me a long time to get over the experience, which meant it took a long time for our family to get over it as well. Looking back, I think that's because I was trying so hard to "get over it." Now that I was well, I wanted to make up for everything I couldn't do while I was away, and especially things for the children. For two years we had a whirlwind of travel, activities, a summer in Israel. It was too much and too quickly.

"You have to take life as it comes," I said in my dream on the

Gripsholm. But that suggests a balance that has never been easy for me to achieve. When I accept a situation, even a very challenging one, I am at my best. In a crisis, I rise to the occasion. But when the situation is unclear, when there is a sense of something more that is demanded but it is not clear exactly what, things are not so easy for me.

Does this go back to the Holocaust? No doubt much of it does. That's when I first discovered that I *could* be stronger and more competent than I ever imagined, certainly as a fifteen-year-old kid. But most of life, thank Heaven, is not so demanding! And what does it mean *then* to rise to the challenge—as a wife, as a friend, above all, as a mother?

It took me many years even to ask myself such questions, and some of that happened while I was still in the hospital. My father visited me a number of times from Los Angeles, and we talked as we never had before. I was entirely honest with him. I told him about decisions of his I agreed with, others with which I did not. It all came out of me. And he was honest in turn, sharing parts of his life and his feelings that he had never discussed with me. We talked about marriage and family and being a parent and being a child. We talked as father and daughter, but also as friends. And talking with him so directly helped me understand a lot of things about my own parenting, and my own children, as well.

These conversations were a turning point, and my father and I remained closest friends through the eight more years that he was to live. As I have described, he was still with us for Vicki's bat mitzvah in 1972—he would never have been anywhere else—and that is part of what makes that memory so sweet. As I have also written, I knew how few of us who survived had *any* parent still alive. I had my father and my aunt. I had been, all these years, one of the "lucky ones."

When I learned he was in the hospital in 1974, I was worried. But he had been hospitalized not long before for the same condition—a heart problem—and I had flown out then. His doctor told me not to come so soon again; it was not necessary. It would just scare him. He would be all right.

And then the call came—to come to Los Angeles as quickly as possible. I was on the plane within hours. By the time I got to the hospital I learned he had died less than an hour before, just as the plane was landing.

My reaction? I was furious. I was angry at him for not waiting for me. For not waiting until I could be with him one last time. This was genuine fury. "Didn't you know I was coming?" A friend waits for a friend. And he didn't wait for me.

I asked for time to be alone with him in the hospital room. I needed the chance to have that conversation. And I made a decision that perhaps echoes a decision I had made so many years ago, within barbed wires, about what I had to do. I decided I would take him with me, that he would be buried in Detroit, that I would take him home. No one gave me permission. But this was what I knew I had to do.

And so our long journey, separate and together, came to this point. From Munkacs to Košice to Teplice-Šanov

to Philadelphia to Detroit to Los Angeles and back to
Detroit again.

"Go my child, go."

No, Father. I will not go. You are coming with me. I am
taking you home.

REUNIONS

The Last of the Mohicans

Wɪᴛʜ ᴛʜᴇ ᴅᴇᴀᴛʜ of my father, I became a "survivor" in the small "s" sense of the word. Although I still had my aunt and cousins from my father's side, I was now the sole survivor of my immediate family, the four of us who had once lived in a small town on a river, with a promenade where everyone watched the world go by. I was, as I said to a friend, "the last of the Mohicans." Zoli had been the same for many years, since no one from his immediate family survived the destruction.

In the late 1970s we also became "survivors" in a more public sense. These were the years in which, seemingly out of nowhere, the Holocaust began to generate much wider interest. There were films, television programs, a flowering of interviews and articles. Suddenly people wanted to talk about it. And we, who had somehow lived through it, became "Holocaust survivors": a title that had acquired (there is no other way to say it) an unexpected cachet.

Of course, the new interest in the Holocaust did *not* come "out of nowhere." Some people, including many survivors, had been working long and hard to document the history of the destruction, to establish memorials, simply to remember. Writers like Elie Wiesel were already well known. But this was still a subject on the periphery, even within the Jewish community. There was nothing like the attention that suddenly emerged.

For myself, I must say that I met these new developments with a mixture of feelings. As I had confided to my diary, in the first days following liberation the crematorium was "our nightmare." My camp sisters and I were "telling everybody about it, whether we want to or not." At that time, talking about it was a compulsion. It was a way of trying to wake up—to convince ourselves that the nightmare really was over—even if we didn't want to go *too* far into it for fear of being swallowed up again. And, of course, being surrounded by interested and compassionate listeners, the wonderful people who were our liberators, made an enormous difference.

Once in America, it was a new situation. "When you laugh, the whole world laughs with you." So that was what most of us tried to do. Still, among ourselves, the topic came up all the time. Almost any conversation with other survivors found a way to lead back to the war: where we were, what we did, how we endured. But we remained, as we would say today, "in the closet." In those years we were not "survivors" but "greeners," trying to establish ourselves, and talking about gas chambers and mass murder was not the way to get ahead. So I scribbled to my diary, remembered in my nightmares, and kept most of it to myself. Once, during the first years in Philadelphia, I was working as a cashier, and someone asked me about the number tattooed on my arm. "What's that?" "It's my phone number," I answered. "I don't want to forget it." And, indeed, I didn't.

Clearly, the wider interest was not there during the earlier years. Still, I cannot blame it all on the outside. I had my own doubts as well. I myself could hardly believe what had occurred. As I wrote in my diary: How could such things be real? How could such things be true? If I myself could hardly grasp it, how could I expect that others would believe it? The truth is that I did not expect them to grasp it. Knowing how hard it was for me, even having lived it, I was certain that *no one* would let themselves believe it.

There was also the fear of personally representing such atrocity. People had seen the newsreels that played so widely after the war—those pictures of naked skeletons, the living and the dead indistinguishable. For most people, those photos—and those skeletons—*were* the "concentration camps." They had little idea that those whom they viewed with horror were once human beings exactly like themselves. And so we survivors asked ourselves: Who would want to stand for such images? Strange as it may seem today, many of us were simply fearful and ashamed. We covered up our vulnerability, our nakedness, with strength and silence and any sign of outward well-being. "Hi, Joe! I'm fine, Joe. *That's* not me! How are *you?*" Who can blame us? We'd already had enough experience representing "things"—inhuman "things" that other people feared.

And then there were the problems of memory itself: not only the pain of remembering, which was bad enough, but the possibility. As I described, in the midst of the destruction, I tried to block out what was going on around me. "That's *not* my mother. That's *not* my family." I did not succeed—I always knew what was happening—but it was as though I knew it through a shade or filter. It was "there," but not entirely "real." Almost all of us did that because, if you allowed yourself to respond to the truth of the situation, you did not last long. Many prisoners died—not only because they were gassed or beaten or shot—but simply because they let themselves see, really see, where fate had brought them.

One result of my "shade" was that I later remembered only certain episodes and fragments—those that made a particular impression, for whatever reason, or broke through my shield. I have told you many of these—the *Scheisskapo* and her vanity, seeing the *Sonderkommando* after they had been shot, the whip that hit both Marika and me. Some of these scenes stand out, perhaps, because they were unusual—not the dull, gray terror that was everyday. Other things stand out, I think, because they were simply impossible to block out: terrified screams, crawling lice, the smell of burning flesh. It is easier to close one's eyes than one's ears, or one's skin.

How does one retell with such a repertoire? I had certain experiences and impressions, but how one thing led to another—all the dates and links—was missing. Yet I should say that a full chronicle was not only impossible for me, but also not of greatest interest. What fascinated me, and still fascinates me, is not outward events, but human responses. How do different people react in such circumstances? How are they changed, and not changed, by the challenges they face? What happens to care, strength, and memory itself when everything is designed to destroy them?

Those were the topics of my "testimony" and my "curriculum" before we used such terms to describe what Holocaust survivors might have to tell and to teach. Still, I hesitated. Who would be interested in listening to this Mohican?

Listeners

MANY MORE WERE interested in listening, I would soon discover, than I had imagined. Although I remained hesitant, I was encouraged especially by John Mames, a friend and survivor (he had been in hiding during the war) who was really the first person in our area to become involved in speaking publicly about the destruction. John was a visionary. For many years he had been committed to the Holocaust being taught in universities and high schools where, at that time, there was almost nothing about it. When, in the late 1970s, the new popular interest in the Holocaust emerged, John was ready. He contacted friends, called meetings, and persuaded many of the rest of us to join him. I was one of his early recruits.

For me, speaking publicly was initially one of those challenges that, however hesitant, I also welcomed. I *wanted* people to know about what happened, and, especially, I wanted young people to know. I didn't know what they would get out of it, but I trusted John's conviction that it would be something. Above all, I wanted to do this for all my dear ones who were killed, my family. There was so little I could do for them at the time. Speaking about it was something I could do now.

I must also say I wanted people to know, or try to know, so that I myself could remember more deeply. It literally takes someone's interest, and someone's questions, to give my own memory life and form. When I am alone, everything tends to remain somewhat vague, more an overall feeling than distinct events. Memories are there, but it is as though they are waiting in the shadows. Undoubtedly, this is another reflection of my "shade." Within it, my mind goes in so many directions and, at the same time, in no single direction. So here, too, I need the focus of a particular goal or challenge. For remembering, I need your questions, the spark of conversation, fully to bring it out. Then memories take their shape and find their words. They emerge between us.

For this reason, I never bring notes or a set speech when I am asked to talk about the Holocaust. At this point I have spoken often enough that I could certainly do that. I will confess that there have been times, when I have committed myself to speak but sensed little genuine interest, that I have gone to "automatic pilot." But then there is no connection—neither with the listener nor even with myself. It's like talking to the air; it's like talking to nobody. This is a topic in which there is enough emptiness already.

So I size up my listeners. I want to know what *they* want to know; really, I *need* to know that in order to begin to speak myself. Then one thought sparks another, and then another, that I may not have even known I had. This is the part that is so gratifying. Whatever I imagine I'm teaching, I'm learning at the same moment. We're learning together.

This is what I have discovered over the years, but it came as a surprise at the beginning, and especially the *degree* of connection that was possible. I remember one high school I visited in the early eighties. It was a large group, several classes put together, but I noticed one young man who seemed distracted. It is interesting that out of all those kids, I would notice this one. Suddenly he got up and left the room. It didn't change anything—the rest of the group had many questions—but I was aware of it. After the session he came back in and walked up to me. He said he wanted me to know that he was an epileptic and had had the first signs of a seizure. So he got up, took his medication, and did what he needed to do. "But I wanted to tell you," he said, "that I stayed near the door so I wouldn't miss anything. I heard everything you said. Thank you very much for coming."

How do you respond to something like that? With a hug, of course, and a gratitude that is more than personal. My sense is that people want to make contact with these experiences when they have a way to do so. For all the fear and resistance that the Holocaust provokes—and those are the *right* reactions to it—there is something about hearing us, touching and being touched by us, that clearly draws people. Just as someone's questions enable me to talk about it, so perhaps hearing a survivor gives form to their own vaguer apprehensions.

One of the things I've noticed is that, at the end of a talk, there are always a few people who come up and ask if they could see my number. I don't think it's morbid curiosity, or maybe this is what "morbid curiosity" means. It seems to be another way for them to allow the destruction to be real, to see with their own eyes a bit of what they had only imagined.

Of course, there have been very bad times as well: being confronted by Holocaust deniers or others who wanted to use our presence for their own, sometimes vicious, agenda. But these experiences have been very rare, and if there has been awkwardness, it has almost always been of the most gentle kind: people being afraid to ask what was really on their minds, or wanting to "do something" for us but not knowing how or what.

At one Catholic school, I could tell that the nuns were deeply touched by what I and another survivor, my friend Alex, had relayed. After the program, Sister Mary came up and nervously handed me a check for seventy-five dollars. "I know it's very little," she said, "but we want in this small token to express our thanks for your coming." I was moved by her gesture. "Sister Mary," I said, "I appreciate your kindness. I am honored by being invited and having the chance to speak with your students. If it is all right with you, what I would like to do is give this in your school's name as a donation to the Holocaust Memorial Center." She was pleased and visibly relieved.

On the drive home, my comrade Alex suddenly said, "Guess what? Sister Mary gave me a check. I told her we do this as an honor and a duty, but I would be very happy to give it as a donation to the Holocaust Memorial Center. That was fine with her."

"Really," I said. "How much did she give you?" Alex sat back. "It was a check for fifty dollars."

"Ha! Mine was for seventy-five!"

What can I say? Suffering has not cleansed me of my pride.

Mind Readers

I FIRST MET Hank Greenspan in 1979. As he describes in his introduction, we were both at a program about survivors' experiences at liberation. I could not contain myself when the social worker, speaking about survivors, repeated that no one "knew how to handle them" in the early years. The "them" was us! Two of "them," myself and another survivor, were sitting next to her on the panel. But it was as though we were still alien beings.

What I remember most about Hank that night was his enthusiasm. When the program ended, he practically sprang out of his chair. "I want to interview you. Can we meet? Can we talk? *When* can we meet?" I have never seen such excitement. "It was like your life depended on it," I told him years later. "In a way," he said, "it did."

Our first interview was a few weeks later, and we ended up meeting every Monday for the next eight months. There was no particular plan, but that became the pattern, and Monday was our day. Usually it was for lunch and three or four hours of talk. There was always more to say. One thought led to another, and I had no idea I even had so many thoughts until they came pouring out in our conversations. It was as though Hank was the listener I had been waiting for; just as, for him, I seemed to be the person whose story he needed to understand.

His compassion was obvious from the beginning, but equally important was that intensity, that needing to know. He wanted to look at things from every side, from every angle, especially the psychological questions that were also of greatest interest to me. What was it like then? What is it like now? How did I get from there to here? And how is "there" still here?

Hank was always gentle, but, at the same time he was tenacious. What did I mean by this? Is this feeling the same as that other? When I first told him about my diary—in which we could read directly my reflections from earlier years—he was most excited of all. I remember translating pages for him, and his constantly stopping me along the way: "Can you read that bit again?" "Can you go back to that earlier section one more time?" It was obvious how much this meant to him.

The longer we worked, the deeper our friendship and our

collaboration became. Somehow we developed a rapport that even now, after twenty-five years, I don't think we understand. We really did seem to read each other's minds. I would start a sentence, and he could finish it. Not that he actually did, but I could see in his eyes that he knew what was coming next, sometimes the exact words. The same was true the other way. I anticipated the questions he would ask, and his questions after those. Was he interviewing me or making it possible for me to interview myself? As I experienced it, the two were the same.

The process of working together was totally involving, but it was not always easy. Every Monday, before Hank arrived, I was wound up—some combination of excitement and anxiety. What would come up? How would it go? Only once, many years after our early meetings, did memory fully overwhelm me. I will talk about that later. But perhaps there was that sense of possible danger, of going too far. That may be why I often got a headache after we met. I am not sure if the headache was from what we talked about or what we didn't talk about. Or perhaps it was from all that one can never talk about. "My pen wants to go on and on by itself," I wrote in my diary. "It is sliding from my hand." Even with the most caring and careful listener, there is always more. That may be just as well.

Still, I wanted to open up as much as I could. Even with the anxiety and the headaches, I wanted to remember. That, again, had to do with the "shade." I remembered only bits and pieces, almost arbitrarily chosen, but not the fuller story with more of the connections. Not having a sense of the whole left me with a sense of holes within myself. It is like having a dream, still experiencing the feeling and the impact of it, but not being able to remember how it unfolded. It is your own experience, and yet you cannot grasp it. I have dreams like that all the time.

Talking with Hank, especially as the years went on, helped me to remember more. Strange to say, I think that also happened because of what he did *not* know. When we survivors talk among ourselves, somehow we always come back to it. "This reminds me of then." "This is what I did." "This is what I saw." We almost fight to be heard, and often that means we only become more lost within ourselves. Each of our stories tends to block out the others. "Yes, I know." "Yes, I was there." "Yes, I had my own experience." With Hank, it was the opposite. As far as direct experience, there was *everything* to tell, to explain, exactly because he did not know, but he so much wished to. So nothing was presumed. Nothing was taken for granted. And that provided both of us the time and space to learn about it, and reflect upon it, together.

There are still gaps; there always will be. There is what remains beyond everyone's grasp, whether one was there or not. There is all that is lost and cannot be restored. But, for me, there are also connections between the dots where there were only dots before. This book, our book, is the completion of my diary that I began so many years ago. As is clear, our work together all this time has also been one of those recreations—of family, of belonging, of purpose—to which I keep returning. Hank says it has been the same for him.

School Reunion

ONE OF THE consequences of my "shade," as I've described, is that I remember only certain episodes from the destruction. Another consequence, and this is more painful, is that I also lost the memory of much of my life before the war. It is as though the veil I drew across the bad experiences cast its shadow on the good as well. And so I see my childhood, too, through a kind of haze. There are certain pictures, overall feelings, and some of the specific memories that I have relayed. But there are also so many gaps—my school subjects, my teachers, the town as a whole—I see it from a very long distance. It's there, but I cannot go back into it, I cannot relive it. It never feels entirely real to me, which has meant, at times, that I do not feel entirely real myself. Knowing who you are, even *that* you are, depends on knowing you come from somewhere, a place you can remember.

In 1981, I traveled to the first World Gathering of Jewish Holocaust Survivors, which was held in Jerusalem. But my real destination was another gathering that was scheduled in Herzliya, on Israel's Mediterranean coast, a few days earlier. This was a reunion of the Hebrew *gymnasium* of Munkacs, where I had been a student for one year. The school had been a center of Jewish life in our town. People were traveling from around the world—the United States, Canada, Australia, South Africa, South America, all over Europe—to participate. Can you imagine? On the coast of Israel, on the other side of the abyss, we were going to have a school reunion.

I went with enormous excitement and enormous fear. How many people would I remember? Who would remember me? Had I ever really been a part of this? Had I ever really been?

The first moments confirmed my worst fears. I didn't remember anyone, and none of their own references sparked any connection. Whatever particular problems I had with memory, I also realized that I was one of the youngest from my town who had survived. I could count those in my age group on one hand. So it was also natural that we would not remember in the same way as people who had been older. They already had a life before the war. We were just kids, barely getting started. "What am I doing here?" I wondered. "This was a terrible mistake." I felt horrible, empty and alone.

Then it started. Someone said, "We are looking for Katz, Agi. Katz, Agi."

"What? Who?" I said, "Oh, that's me! That's me!" Somebody remembered me. "You mean, you remember me?"

"Of course, of course. Everything you did."

I was revitalized. Almost literally, I was reborn. People remembered things, small things, childhood things, school things. "You won the first prize and I hated you for it. Because I won the second."

"What? Where? How?" She sent me the picture.

Just as with my memories of the war, I knew these things happened, but I was not able to retrieve them on my own. Here, too, I needed someone to help me bring them out. One thing led to another, and then more and more.

The next day it was like shadows coming out of the shadows. I met one of my teachers. I went up to her and I started shaking her. I said, "Are you *sure* you taught me? Are you sure?" She said, "Oh Agika, did I teach you? You were one of my favorite pupils!" I saw another teacher who had always been one of the most demanding, a perfectionist for us as for himself. He could be intimidating, although we always knew he cared. I went up to him and said, "You know, I used to be so scared of you! But, you know, you're not so scary anymore!"

For three days and nights hardly any of us slept or ate. We were that wound up, finding each other, retrieving fragments of a community's life that most of us thought were gone forever.

We were joined by other survivors from Munkacs, not only those who had been part of the *gymnasium*, and it was as though for three days and nights we recreated the life of our city. That, at one time, there was this Jewish town that existed. We belonged to it, and it belonged to us. For three days and nights we were again Mohicans. And we allowed ourselves to imagine, in our excitement, that it would go on, that we were not the last.

Of course, we *were* the last. The city did *not* belong to us—certainly not anymore, if it ever really did. And we did not belong to it either, as we had learned that day at the brick factory when only the Ukrainian boy who played the harmonica came to take a final look.

So we returned to earth. Or perhaps, we departed again. Personally, when I got home, I was very glad that I had gone. It confirmed that there *was* a life, including my life, before. But when I looked at the photos from the reunion, I could barely remember who was who, who was married, who had children, almost none of the details. Once again, the specifics evaded my memory. But at least I remembered the gathering itself—I remembered being remembered—and, under the circumstances, that was reunion enough.

Revisiting Marco

REUNIONS. WHEN SOMETHING cannot be retrieved—either because it has been forgotten or, more profoundly, because it has been lost—we improvise. An aunt becomes a mother. Her niece, or grandniece, becomes her child. A hospital ward, even an ant farm, become miniatures of the world. A community that no longer exists recreates itself for three days and nights. One grave becomes a substitute for another. Soon after my father's funeral, a friend came up to me: "I must tell you, I was glad to go to your father's grave. I felt that my father is there, too. Would you allow me to visit there?" "I would be very glad to share it with you," I said.

Some of the improvising we do ourselves. But you also have to be lucky. There needs to be a listener, a grave, or a special person to help you to remember, mourn, or be reborn.

As I have described, in the first days after liberation, that person was Marco. The shelter that I sought in the dream of my mother's protection was recreated under Marco's care. Incredibly, as I look back at my diary, it was only a few days before my sense of belonging to the world was restored. There would be many difficult times ahead, but this was the beginning. The attentiveness of Marco and our other liberators was responsible for it, and it was the basis upon which I rebuilt my life.

As I wrote, before leaving the hospital Marco and I promised to stay in touch and eventually meet in Israel, where he was going. During the years I was still in Europe and during my first years in the U.S. we exchanged many letters, and he continued to be my guide. Even in Philadelphia—and especially during the most difficult times—I was still thinking about going to Israel, but he discouraged me from coming. The war for Israeli independence, the hardships and the dangers of making a new country, were more than he wanted me to go through after everything else. Eventually we agreed to meet there at a later time. And we each became more and more involved in making our lives where we were.

It was not until 1968, the trip to Israel that followed my hospitalization, that Marco and I had our reunion. It had been twenty-three years since we had seen each other, when, having provided a horse and buggy, he saw me off to Prague and the rest of my life.

Now our families could also meet—Zoli and Marco became good friends—and we continued to visit through the years. We became part of each other's lives again, and it was wonderful.

One very special visit was seeing Marco during the week of the World Gathering in 1981. My camp sisters, Marika and Mignon, were with me, along with their husbands. In a quiet moment, each of the husbands thanked Marco for restoring their wives to life, thus making possible all the happiness that would follow. Their gratitude was deeply felt, and I will never forget the image of Marco: proud as a peacock, taking in what it meant for us to be together—he, the three camp sisters, their husbands, all of us with children—having reached that moment.

I especially remember this image because such pride and fulfillment were, sadly, rare for Marco during the years after the war. Despite all the nurture and encouragement he could provide for others, he could not do the same for himself. The destruction and much that had come later had left him embittered. Unlike me with my shade, he could not keep away the things he had seen and, beyond that, he could not shake the immensity of everyone and everything that had been lost. For him, there was no celebration in the aftermath. Although he had an important job in Israel, a family and grandchildren, none of it seemed to balance the heaviness he carried, which became greater as the years went on. When he eventually developed a serious heart condition, it was obvious to everybody who knew him that he was not taking care of himself; he was letting himself go. Not everyone finds a way to "improvise." Or, hard as it is to write, perhaps dying can also be a form of "reunion."

Marco died seven years after the Jerusalem gathering. When I was next in Israel, about a year after his death, I went with his wife to his grave. It was good to have at least this way to visit him again. And yet, had it been entirely up to Marco, there would not have been even this bit of ground where he—the brilliant, compassionate, and haunted individual that he was—could be remembered. Sometime after the funeral, a will of his was found. It was too late to change anything. He had wanted to be cremated.

Reflections

REFLECTIONS. WE ARE drawn toward both the future and the past, but they have different weight for each of us. Some dwell more in what was, both the good times and their destruction. Others think more about the future, what we are trying to create, and to recreate.

The relationship between past and future also changes at different times in our lives. Some periods are dominated by memory. Some by anticipation. Sometimes the future stands against the past, promising renewal. Sometimes the future is foreboding, the terror of the terror's return. Either way, one world reminds you of the other. New experiences reflect old ones. They put them in a different light, or a different darkness.

I became a grandmother in 1988, and that role is very much the center of my life. There are now seven—Vicki's five and Amy's two—and each has his or her very specific style. Here are some of my loves:

Rivky, the first, is poetic, reflective, strikingly mature—as eldests are supposed to be! If she has a problem with Vicki, she'll call me. "Nana, will you have a talk with your daughter?" Like Marika and I so many years ago, she needs, at times, a mediator.

Shmuel is smart, serious, analytic, and observant. He is gifted and he knows it, and so he can also be a bit competitive with the others.

Moshe is the love of my life, the light in his eyes lights my heart. He is hearing impaired, and we were initially worried about how this might affect him. But he is handling it beautifully.

Devora is a little princess—demure, outspoken, moody at times. "Sarah Bernhardt," as the saying goes—she knows how to get a response.

Miriam, Vicki's youngest, is a little chatterbox. She is very smart, very quick, and very funny. She also knows how to take over the room.

Justin, Amy's first, is warm, polite, and easygoing—a different rhythm, a different style—and he is a beautiful boy.

Jeremy, her second, is a *mazik*. He is perpetual motion, into everything, regardless of who or what might be in the way.

I cannot measure love. It is not shared or subdivided. Each

of the grandchildren gets it for who they are. And love for each replenishes love for the others.

I am reminded of my own grandfather, my mother's father. This is one of those memories that has stayed with me. In 1943 the grandchildren—my cousins and I—were visiting my grandparents in Tiszaujlak, where my mother was raised. My mother and her two sisters—Olga and Margitka—were taking a few days to visit their brother, my Uncle Bandi, who lived in Budapest. As it turns out, this was the last time the four of them would be together. Bandi lived the high life, and he wanted his three sisters to have a real holiday, which they did. We kids were dropped off at the grandparents', who were doing the babysitting.

My grandfather was a very formal, patriotic Hungarian gentleman—one whose actions were disciplined and deliberate. And I remember that he took all the grandchildren into the backyard, lined us up, and spoke about each grandchild in turn. He began with me, the oldest.

"This one I love. How can I help but love her? She is my first. She is my number one.

"And this one is bad like the devil! But, boy, is he smart! He can outsmart me anytime. How can I not love him?

"This one is as dumb as they come. But she is gorgeous, gorgeous, gorgeous! And I love her.

"This one will be a professor! I will have to respect him. So how can I not love him, too?"

This was in 1943, not long before the Germans took over Hungary, which was the real beginning of the end. One year later, only my Aunt Margitka and I would be alive.

For Margitka, too, one set of grandchildren reminds her of the other. They kindle her reflections and ignite her love.

The Wind

FIFTY YEARS AFTER that last family reunion in Tiszaujlak:
It is April 1993, the official opening of the United States
Holocaust Memorial Museum in Washington. As everyone
who was there remembers, it was a cold, wet, brutally windy
day. The Mall, stretching out behind the new museum, was a
field of mud. Umbrellas were blown inside-out. We survivors,
our families, and our friends were gathered—an assembly under
umbrellas that were themselves survivors; or, for the inventive,
green plastic garbage bags. We were, indeed, a motley collection.
"We're back at *Zehlappel*"—morning roll call—was the repeated

one-liner, the recurring reflection.

In Birkenau, however, there was no army band playing for us, at least not one from our side. Certainly there was no President Clinton to greet us. In Birkenau, Elie Wiesel did not have a place at the podium, even if the wind that day forced him to grab it with both hands and dodge the periodic blowdown of falling flags.

Before the museum and the other memorials that have been established in recent years, we had no place to go to remember. For years I saw my mother floating in the air, in the smoke, in the wind, and I couldn't reach her. I couldn't bring her down. The museums and the memorials are both for them, our dear ones, and for us. Like good listeners, they help bring out our memories and give them form. Like graves, they provide a place to revisit and to mourn. Like close friends, they provide a way to share our memories together.

Still, I must tell you candidly that this is also improvisation, and we know it. We want to believe that our families and communities did not die in vain, totally without meaning, simply eliminated. We want to believe that there will be some impact from all of this—the museums and the memorials—even if we don't know what it is. We want to feel that they are *somewhere,* and that what happened to them is somewhere, and not simply erased without memory or care.

We want to believe all of this, and most of us do. The museums and memorials, and especially that museum and memorial, also provide a kind of reunion. Even as we are reminded that it is cold and it is raining and the wind still blows.

Permanent Exhibit

Not all reunions are welcome. Inside the museum, I had an experience that was one of the few times, outside of a nightmare, that I actually relived a scene from the Holocaust. It was certainly the first time that Hank had seen me remember in this way, even after fourteen years of our talking together.

We were going through the exhibit the day after the official opening. I must tell you that, in general, I felt very little during most of the tour. I appreciated the work that had been done—the care, the historical detail, the architecture of the building, which is overwhelming. At one point, in the section about Auschwitz,

I had the odd experience of thinking I was hearing my own voice. "How strange," I thought. "I am imagining that I can hear myself speaking." And suddenly I realized that I *was* hearing myself speaking. Part of one of my interviews plays in that section, along with the testimonies of other Auschwitz survivors. So there I was, standing in the Auschwitz exhibit, listening to my own memories of that place.

I met myself again at the end. I am one of a dozen survivors who appear in the video, *Testimony*, that plays continually at the conclusion of the permanent exhibit. Here, too, I cannot tell you that I was terribly moved, although I thought the filmmaker did an excellent job. A number of people who have been to the museum—and this still happens to me today—will see me somewhere and insist that we have met before. Most of the time it is because they recognize me from the video in the Washington museum. That first visit, I also recalled a young schoolgirl who had heard me speak at our local Holocaust center in Detroit a few years earlier. She was a very nice kid, and she said that next time she would also like to bring her mother to visit me. It was obvious from the way she said it that she thought that I, along with the rest of the Holocaust, lived in the museum. So this was not the first time I experienced myself as part of the "permanent exhibit."

It was not my voice, or the video, that brought things back. It was midway through, turning a corner and seeing the railroad car, the "cattle car," that stands in the center of that section. For whatever reason, it was *this* that got to me. This object in the middle of the museum tore through the years, and tore through me, and brought me back. For me, it was not simply a "cattle car." It was *that* "cattle car," waiting for me all this time. Everything and everyone else disappeared. I was entirely paralyzed. My knees started to give way. It was as though I could see vividly our little group—my mother, my aunt, my little brother—in the far right corner of the car, just where we had been. They were still inside, and I could not move. I could not do anything.

At the same time, there appeared to be no way to go to the next section of the exhibit without walking through the car. Later, realizing other survivors had had difficulty here, the museum created another pathway. But, at the time, there seemed to be no choice.

I closed my eyes. I did not want to see them there. I did not want to go through, but I knew that I had to. Zoli and Hank were both with me, and they each took one of my arms and supported me. I kept my eyes closed, and together the three of us literally ran through the car, with me carried along between them. Once I was on the other side, once I was through, it was as though it had all been a dream. I was safe. I was with the two of them. I had come back to life, to *this* life, and I had no more difficulties that afternoon in the museum.

Looking back, I am still not certain why it was this that got to me. Indeed, I ask myself why didn't I want to see my family again—my dear ones, those who were everything to me? Why didn't I reach out? Wasn't this the reunion I had wished for?

I think it is simply this: I knew where the car was going. I knew the fate that awaited them. I knew there was no escape, no safety, no exit. As much as I missed them, as much as I still yearn for them, I could not bear to see their terror. I could not bear to see them disappear into nothingness again. I simply could not bear it.

The Most Beautiful on Earth

EVERY REUNION BRINGS the possibility of renewed separation, of renewed loss. We recreated our little city at the school reunion in Israel, and then we lost it all again. I found Marco, my liberator and dear friend, and I lost him again. I saw my family in the cattle car, and I could not bear to lose them again.

It is an old theme. As I wrote in my diary in 1950, in Philadelphia: "I knew we should get out of my hometown because it would be Russian. And I also knew that in my hometown, where I lived my sweetest, happiest time, that life would never return. I wanted to escape from the memories because

I didn't want to live through, first the good, then the miserable destroying of life." In formal interviews—not the ones with Hank, but for projects like Steven Spielberg's Shoah Foundation and others—they always organize the questions into "before," "during," and "after." But the way we live our lives, and the ways we remember, are never divided into such compartments.

One more loss occurred most recently. Shortly after this manuscript was completed, my Aunt Margitka died. As I have described, she was the most important person in my life outside my immediate family. She represented my mother whom I had lost, just as I was her child. She was the proud grandmother whom my own children didn't have, but *did*—thanks to her. Perhaps most important, she was my closest friend. We shared everything—our thoughts, our hopes, our regrets—and I couldn't talk with anyone the way I could talk with her. She was as smart as anyone I've known, and as funny, and she told me exactly what she thought. It was not always easy to hear, but I knew I could count on the truth as she saw it—which, most of the time, simply turned out to be the truth.

The loss of her own children was always with her, but she had a full life in Israel. She lived in the same apartment in Tel Aviv from 1948, the birth of the country, until she died. She traveled often, seeing us in the States, going on vacations with us, or all of us visiting her there. She and four other women— they called themselves "the girls"—had for years been meeting once or twice a week for lunch and cards. Although she was the oldest, everyone thought of her as the youngest because of her spirit and her wit. Up until the last months, she baked for them, and it was painful for her, toward the end, when she could no longer be the hostess. Still, "the girls" all came to her apartment. It was not for the baking.

The last time I saw her alive, she was already failing badly. I was wearing a purple outfit. And she kept staring at me and saying, "I love that color," "I love that color," "I *love* that color." For whatever reason, that purple became, in those moments, the most beautiful thing on earth. When I returned to Israel again, for the unveiling of her gravestone, I wore the same purple outfit. I wanted to bring her the most beautiful thing on earth.

She had arranged her own reunion. On her gravestone, her own name was engraved, along with the names of the two children she had lost so many years before—Liluci and Zoli—the most beautiful and beloved on earth.

Words

"Survivor," "Testimony," "Legacies"—these are the words that now describe who we are, what we remember, what we have to pass on. They are the official words—words for gatherings, public ceremonies, special occasions. As important as such words can be, I have never been comfortable with them.

Even "survivor." I am *not* "a Survivor" with a capital "S." Perhaps this is my own oversensitivity, but I always feel that turning us into "Survivors" makes us unreal again. Like the people in the newsreels, our loved ones, we also become creatures from another planet. Of course, many of us have things in common. But, in the end, the most important thing we have in common is only that we are the ones who are still here. That is the literal meaning of being a "survivor," and it may also be the most reliable.

"Testimony." As I described, for me, memory is born in conversation. It is not a onetime event, recorded for posterity, put in the museum, and that's the end of it. It is true that we make the tapes with the thought that someone may be interested when we are not here. But I do not talk to "future generations"—at least not yet! I talk with the particular people in front of me. Everything that happens, happens between us. It is not more than that. And it is not less.

"Legacies." Perhaps I am haunted by this one most of all. We who were there know how limited can be *any* parent's ability to prepare the younger generation for what can happen. We know that terribly well. Still, we tend to question ourselves. Were we too protective or not protective enough? Should we have guided them more or let them learn from their own mistakes, and their own successes? This goes for our own children. But we also ask it in a much wider way. Have we done enough? Have we said enough? Have we justified the pure accident of our survival?

We ask it; I ask it. But then I also think of my own parents, the legacy that I myself received. And I realize it is made up of so many small things that turned out to be precious to *me:* things that I gathered up as much because I needed them as because my parents wanted me to have them. I barely remember my mother's face. But I remember her care, her love, and her principles—certain ways one tries to live one's life. Maybe that is why I tried so hard to keep "my lady," Marika's mother, alive. This was what my mother would have done. In trying to do what she would do, I was also trying to keep her with me as my guide. And, looking back, I see that I *have* kept her with me, in that terrible year and in all the years that have followed.

My father was with me through much more of my life; it was a full, mature relationship, as I have described. And yet, when I think of him, I remember certain moments. I remember the way he sang *"En K'elohenu,"* one of our Jewish prayers. Whenever I am at the synagogue, I hear his voice. At certain prayers or hymns, I remember how much joy he got out of singing that particular one. And when it comes up, he is again with me, and I am singing with him. It is the harmony of voices that makes the legacy, the way I tune myself to him, and feel his spirit still singing, through my own voice. Even now, we are singing together.

So, actually, what is a "legacy"? It's these small things that are taken up by those who follow. I can provide whatever I can provide. But, in the end, my legacy is not up to me. It is up to whomever comes after, to pick up this bit, remember that part, find harmony with whatever note, as it may apply to their own circumstances, which I know will be different from mine. You will take what you choose, what you need, just as I did. I can only wish you well, and wish you peace.

So one last time in these pages, I remember my mother's wave. And I repeat what she said to me, as she looked across the mud and the agony, trying to get my attention, trying to imagine a future, trying to invoke hope, trying to bestow the only blessing that, in the end, this world allows:

"Go, my child, go."

Go, my beloved children and grandchildren. Go, my dear comrades and friends. Go, my kind listeners and readers.

Go.

Mother's side of family in Tiszaujlak, mid-1930s

Standing (l. to r.): Peter Kereszturi (Agi's uncle, killed in Auschwitz), Ilonka Katz (Agi's mother, killed in Auschwitz), Irene Kereszturi (Peter's wife, killed in Auschwitz), Bumi Katz (Agi's father), Margitka Goldstein (Agi's aunt), Artur Goldstein (Margitka's husband), Olga Kereszturi (Agi's aunt, killed in Auschwitz), Alizka Kereszturi (Bandi's wife, killed in Auschwitz), Bandi Kereszturi (Agi's uncle, killed in Auschwitz). Seated middle: Jenny Kereszturi (Agi's maternal grandmother, killed in Auschwitz), Samuel Kereszturi (Agi's maternal grandfather, died in 1943). Seated front: Zoli Goldstein (Margitka's son, killed in Auschwitz), Agi.

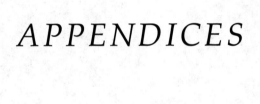

APPENDICES

APPENDICE

1. For Teachers and Students

"Go." That is the way Agi ends *Reflections*, and that is the way it must end. It is now up to us.

These notes are for those who may want to pursue some of the topics raised in these pages. My goal is to suggest sources of particular relevance, but I must emphasize that the list is *very* selective. Certainly it is not a bibliography for the Holocaust in general, which alone would require a volume many times the size of this one. Particularly in the areas of Holocaust history, the role of the Holocaust in public memory, and the representation of the Holocaust in literature and film, there is an enormous body of scholarly work. Among historians, Raul Hilberg, Saul Friedlander, Christopher Browning, Omer Bartov, Deborah Dwork, and many others continue to make essential contributions. Among those who write about the representation of the Holocaust in public memory and in literature, the seminal work of Alvin Rosenfeld, Lawrence Langer, Geoffrey Hartmann, James Young, and Sara Horowitz is barely a beginning. Here, however, I have limited myself to sources that have a much more direct connection with this memoir: the reflections of other survivors that, in my view, resonate or contrast most evocatively with Agi's own.

Even within that limited category, this remains very much *my* list—some of the resources that I have found most compelling during the thirty years that I have been teaching and writing about survivors. Other teachers would compile entirely different lists. Each selection would reflect what has become the legacy of Holocaust survivors for *them*.

MEMOIRS

I rarely use the word "testimonies" to describe survivors' accounts, written or spoken, although that is the term one hears most often. Still, like Agi, I am not comfortable with it. "Testimonies" are formal declarations of witness or of faith: deliberate accounts created "for posterity." Important as they may be, testimonies are only one of the forms in which survivors remember. For remembrance born in the intimacy of conversation, including the conversation between a writer and a page, I prefer more everyday terms like "retelling" or "recounting" or, indeed, "reflections." To say it more glibly—probably too glibly—friends do not "give testimony" to friends.

If you read more than one survivor's account, as I certainly hope you will, you will discover how varied they are in voice, emphasis, and tone. This should not be surprising. Although the destruction was inflicted on its victims as members of groups, it is remembered and retold by individuals. And if Holocaust survivors often say "we," each survivor says "we" in his or her particular way.

Along with Agi, Primo Levi has been my primary teacher about the experience of living through and after the Holocaust. His *Survival in Auschwitz* (originally published in English as *If This Is a Man* in 1959) and his last book, *The Drowned and the Saved* (1988), have no equals. Levi's *The Reawakening* (1965) and *Moments of Reprieve* (1979) have also been essential sources for me. Levi's dream of the "unlistened-to story," which he first discusses in *Survival in Auschwitz*, bears direct comparison with Agi's dream of recurrently finding and losing the security of her mother's lap. I am often asked, by busy readers, to recommend one book about the Holocaust. *Survival in Auschwitz* has always been my choice.

Elie Wiesel is unquestionably the best-known survivor-writer in the United States, and his *Night* (1960) remains a searing and important account. His essay collections *Legends of Our Time* (1968), *One Generation After* (1970), and *A Jew Today* (1978) have also been central in my own thinking. There is much in *Reflections* that resonates with *Night*—especially the dissolution of a childhood and the vow to save an older person (for Agi, "my lady"; for Elie, his father). At the same time, the differences between their accounts are equally noteworthy—especially those concerning gender, religiosity, and the span of time involved (*Night* ends at liberation). For students and for teachers, the differences should prove to be as informative as the similarities.

I would also mention three other memoirs of Auschwitz—all by women—that both complement and contrast with *Reflections*. Charlotte Delbo's *None of Us Will Return* (1968) is, like *Reflections*, written as a series of short, distinct snapshots: in this case, a view of Auschwitz as experienced by a woman who was a French political prisoner. There is probably no other writer who more vividly describes the sensory experience of terror—the cold, the stench, the mud, the thirst, the meaning (and lack of meaning) of the spring sun.

Isabella Leitner also writes in short reflections. Her *Fragments of Isabella* (1978) and *Saving the Fragments* (1985) have since been combined into a single volume, *Isabella: From Auschwitz To Freedom* (2000). Leitner's memories—particularly, the centrality of holding on to her "camp sisters" (who were her actual sisters in Leitner's case) and the themes of nurture and belonging more generally—resonate with Agi's, as my students often note.

Gerda Weissman Klein has become well known from the television documentary *One Survivor Remembers* (1996). Her original memoir *All But My Life* (1957) was one of the earliest women's memoirs published in English—preceding in English both Wiesel's *Night* and Levi's *Survival in Auschwitz*—and it remains an enormously compelling account. Both Gerda and Agi are featured in the video, *Testimony,* that plays at the end of the permanent exhibit in the United States Holocaust Memorial Museum. Here, too, their different sensibilities and styles make an interesting contrast.

Once again, this is only the barest and most selective beginning. Even if one were to limit oneself to memoirs of women who survived Birkenau, the list would be a very long one.

IN PERSON, ON TAPE, IN FILM, ON THE INTERNET

In the 1970s, when I first began interviewing survivors, it was not uncommon for me to hear and read "the survivors are all dying"—precisely the same phrase we hear today, three decades later. When I met Agi in 1979, she was seven years younger than I am today. I hope I am not on the edge of demise; it is clear that Agi is not.

Of course, one cannot argue with demography. In recent years we have, indeed, started to lose survivors in greater and greater numbers. Sixty years after liberation, even the youngest survivors are entering their seventies. No, they are not immortal. But it is realistic to expect that, for more than a decade, there will still be many survivors who can and will publicly retell what they remember. Students and teachers should take every possible opportunity to hear them. Elie Wiesel once said that the truth can only be passed "from eye to eye, from mouth to ear." No memoir, video, or work of art will ever substitute for direct conversation.

There are now tens of thousands of survivors' accounts on videotape. The vast majority of them will be viewed by only a handful of people—in most cases, only by members of survivors' immediate families. Large archives that are well indexed—like the Fortunoff collection at Yale, the collection at the United States Holocaust Memorial Museum, and the Survivors of the Shoah Visual History archive—will be selectively used by researchers.

But, even from these collections, only a small fraction of the testimonies will ever be reviewed.

Video testimony may be most useful for teachers when a survivor can visit the class after the students have seen his or her tape. This relieves survivors of the burden of summarizing their "stories" during class itself (when there is never enough time), and the whole period can then be devoted to direct dialogue. As Agi emphasizes, memory and reflections are born in conversation. In my view, the more such conversation in a class visit, the more worthwhile it will be—for *both* students and survivors.

When there is no opportunity to speak with a survivor directly, I would recommend documentaries that include excerpts from survivors' recounting rather than a single "video testimony." Controversial as it remains, Claude Lanzmann's *Shoah* (1985) contains some of the most extraordinary recording of survivors' retelling that we have, while including the memories of perpetrators, bystanders, and a range of other commentators as well (including the omnipresent Lanzmann himself— prodding, pushing, entrapping—which is part of what makes the film controversial). Only a rare class or individual will have the dedication to view all of *Shoah*'s eleven hours. Even though its length—especially the length of its silences—is part of its power, selections can be made. Two excerpts I often use are the accounts of Filip Muller, who had been a member of the Birkenau *Sonderkommando*, recalling the night the Terezin family camp was gassed, and a brief segment near the film's conclusion in which Warsaw resistance survivor Yitzhak Zuckerman provides what may be the starkest commentary on "living after" that has ever been recorded.

The Thames documentary *Genocide* (1975), program XX of the British *World at War* series, also contains extraordinary excerpts from survivors. These include a brief clip from an interview with Primo Levi—a rare glimpse of the young Levi on film—and a more extended excerpt from Rivka Yosselevska, whose memories of a mass shooting near Pinsk stunned listeners at the Eichmann trial in 1961. Although its narrative may be overly focused on Himmler and the SS, *Genocide* remains one of the best single short documentaries about the Holocaust as a whole, notwithstanding all that have been produced since it appeared. (Teachers will need to be careful not to confuse this Holocaust documentary with another, also called *Genocide*, produced by the Simon Wiesenthal Center in the 1990s. The two are very different works.)

The Shoah Visual History Foundation has created a series of documentaries that include selections from the video testimonies gathered for that project. One of the best, in my view, and the one most relevant to *Reflections*, is *The Last Days* (1998), which retells the fate of Hungarian Jewry.

There are now many interviews with survivors—transcripts, audio, and video—that can be directly accessed on the Internet. One of the more interesting sites includes transcripts and audio recordings of interviews that psychologist David Boder conducted with survivors in 1946, a year after liberation (http://voices. iit.edu/index.html). Recently there has been a wave of interest in early recounting, and Boder's interviews have received a good deal of attention.

Boder's work was unique because his interviews with survivors were the first that were electronically recorded. At the same time, there were immense efforts to gather survivors' written accounts during the first years after liberation. Many of these projects were based in historical commissions founded and directed by survivors themselves. Several thousand written testimonies were collected between 1944 and 1947. I have summarized some of this early recounting in a paper that also includes a discussion of Agi's diary (http://www.ushmm.org/research/center/publications/occasional/2001-02/paper.pdf).

Finally, I would mention one other source that is visual but not testimonial: *The Auschwitz Album* in which Agi found the photo of herself. Published in 1981, the book itself is now out of print. But its story and about half of the photos that the album contained can be found at the website of Yad Vashem, Israel's central Holocaust memorial (http://www1.yadvashem.org/exhibitions/album_auschwitz/home_auschwitz_album.html).

The particular photo that includes Agi happens not to be among the ones on the site. Those that are there also gaze back at us from the other side of the mirror, each trying to tell a story that we will never hear.

—Henry Greenspan

Works Noted

Memoirs and Essays

Delbo, Charlotte. 1968. *None of Us Will Return*. Translated by John Githens. Boston: Beacon Press. [This edition is out of print. The memoir, along with two additional sets of reflections by Delbo, can now be found in *Auschwitz and After*, translated by Rosette C. Lamont. (New Haven: Yale University Press, 1997).]

Klein, Gerda Weissman. 1957. *All But My Life*. New York: Hill and Wang. [An expanded edition was published by Hill and Wang in 1995.]

Leitner, Isabella. 1978. *Fragments of Isabella*. New York: Crowell.

————. 1985. *Saving the Fragments*. New York: Plume. [As noted, both of Leitner's memoirs are now available together as *Isabella: From Auschwitz To Freedom*. New York: Xlibris, 2000.]

Levi, Primo. 1959. *If This Is a Man*. Translated by Stuart Woolf. New York: Orion. [Available in several editions as *Survival in Auschwitz*.]

————. 1965/1986. *The Reawakening*. Translated by Stuart Woolf. New York: Summit Books.

————. 1979. *Moments of Reprieve*. Translated by Ruth Feldman. New York: Summit Books.

————. 1988. *The Drowned and the Saved*. Translated by Raymond

Rosenthal. New York: Simon & Schuster.

Wiesel, Elie. 1960. *Night.* Translated by Stella Rodway. New York: Hill & Wang. [*Night* is available in a number of editions.]

————. 1968. *Legends of Our Time.* Translated by Steven Donadio. New York: Holt, Rinehart, Winston.

————. 1970. *One Generation After.* Translated by Lily Edelman and Elie Wiesel. New York: Random House.

————. 1978. *A Jew Today.* Translated by Marion Wiesel. New York: Random House.

FILMS

Genocide (1975). VHS (1983). Directed by John Pett, David Elstein. Volume XX of the *World at War* series. Thames television.

One Survivor Remembers (1996) VHS. Directed by Kary Antholis. Direct Cinema Limited.

Shoah (1985) VHS. Directed by Claude Lanzmann. Les Films Aleph. [The complete text of *Shoah* was originally published by Pantheon in 1986 and is now available from DaCapo.]

The Last Days (1998) VHS. Directed by James Moll. Survivors of the Shoah Foundation. Universal Studios.

2. Notes on Co-authorship

Reflections is a genuinely co-authored memoir, the result of an intensive, twenty-five year collaboration in which the book emerged "between" Agi and myself. As I suggested in the Introduction, the details of that collaboration both elucidate the form and development of these pages and raise wider questions about memoir, memory, and even authorship itself. These notes are for readers interested in those issues.

How, then, can the memoir of one person be written by two people? Several times in *Reflections*, Agi repeats the notion that "memory is born in conversation." Clearly, however, that is not always the case, nor was it always the case for her. When she wrote about her experiences immediately at liberation, and returned to her journal in later years, she did not need a collaborator. Indeed, some memories seemed to demand expression regardless of conversational context. "The crematorium is our nightmare," she wrote at liberation. "We are telling everybody about it, whether we want to or not." At these times, memories seemed to be telling themselves.

More broadly, Agi's diary itself served as her listener, in both early and later years. At times she directly addressed it as a companion, as diarists often do: "Yes, my Diary, here I am—in

America!" she exclaimed, writing in Philadelphia on the fifth anniversary of the liberation. Most often, Agi addresses herself in her diary. "What do you want, my soul, if I can call you that?" Within our conversations, such reflexive questions remained typical of Agi. "Why would I see things that way?" she would ask, as much to herself as to me. "Does it all go back to that one terrible year? Is that why I make the connection?" Thus, it would not be precisely accurate to say that, within our interviews, an "internal dialogue" became an external one—at least initially. It is rather that Agi brought her internal conversation *into* the conversation between us. On one level, this simply meant that she voiced it aloud, allowing me to be its witness. On another level, of course, it was an invitation to participate—to ask, for example: "What *is* the connection you are making here? How do *you* understand it?"

This sort of reflecting back is the real beginning of an interview, a conversation between two people working hard to understand the perspective of one of them. If an interview is particularly worthwhile, the result of that hard work is that the interviewee's self-understanding is not only clarified; it may also be significantly transformed. This happens in all our most engaged and engaging conversations. Within the most memorable such experiences, we may find ourselves saying: "This is the first time I ever thought about that" or "I never saw it that way before" or "I haven't remembered that in years" or "I hadn't remembered that at all." Memories are often "born in conversation," both their content and their significance, and not only for

Holocaust survivors.

In a good interview, then, people learn things—the interviewee as much as the interviewer. Perhaps because of the interviewing we see in popular media, our usual notion of interviews is far more impoverished. Most typically, we imagine that interviewees have some stable collection of thoughts and memories "stored up" inside of them, and the interviewer simply needs to insert the right question to get them out—something like using a vending machine, or drawing blood. The only dangers, in such a model, are that the interviewer will "get in the way" or "impose something" that taints the outpouring.

Of course, it *is* possible to "get in the way" or "impose something." But those are the least of the challenges that interviewing presents, and also the least suggestive of its process and promise. A good interview is a genuine voyage of discovery. Far from extracting information that is already "stored," such an interview may lead to thoughts and connections between thoughts that are entirely new. This is not because something is "imposed," but because the process of putting thoughts into words, and working with another to find the most elucidating words, is an inherently creative one. That is part of what makes a good interview so engaging, even about painful experiences. Neither the interviewer nor the interviewee knows ahead of time precisely what the words will be or where they may lead. Together, they may find their way to insights that neither one of them could have predicted beforehand or arrived at alone. As Agi described: "One thought sparks another, and then another, that I did not even know I had. That is the part that is so gratifying. Whatever I'm teaching, I'm learning at the same moment. We're learning together."

This memoir was co-authored, then, because the twenty-five years of interviews on which it is based were themselves co-authored—the mutually creative process that is inherent in sustained and deepening conversation. Certainly, our roles in those conversations were different. But the shape that memories took, and the words they found, depended on both of us.

Some degree of co-authorship characterizes all good interviews—even one-time encounters. That is what makes interviews *inter*views, as opposed to soliloquies or forced confessions. At the same time, there are also more specific reasons why retelling horrific memories may depend on the presence of an engaged and responsive listener. To say it most directly, some things may simply be too terrifying to remember in isolation. In those circumstances, a listener serves both to receive and to contain what is being recalled. For many Holocaust survivors, remembering without such a listener may not be possible.

This was true for Agi even in those first days of liberation, when memories seemed to be pouring out on their own. Although she wrote about "telling everybody about the crematoria," there is no description of the crematoria in her diary itself. Indeed, she recalls deliberately avoiding these memories in her writing. Discussing her early pages, she noted that "even here, between me and the paper, I would not go into it. I could not. I was telling it to others. But I could not tell it to myself."

A year after liberation, waking from an Auschwitz nightmare, Agi's extraordinary "Haunting Horror" entry expressed both the insistence of memory and the impossibility of remembering alone. Having begun to list staccato images of the destruction—fire, bones, suffocated innocents—she continues: "My pen wants to go on and on, by itself. It is sliding from my hand. At times like this my strength leaves me. It leaves me each time I see it all again. It leaves me when I see the truth once more." The first time we discussed this entry, Agi reflected further about both the demands of Holocaust memories and the risks of facing them in isolation. "One world reminds you of the other," she reiterated. "But you don't want to pull yourself so fully into the deepness that you feel you cannot get out. That's when you need someone to help bring you out of it. It's easy to say, 'Well, you have to help yourself.' You *can't* always help yourself."

Thus, a second reason why some memories are "born in conversation": these memories are too painful to be borne alone. Even with a responsive listener there are limits. The very form through which memories are approached in these pages—a series of discrete reflections—is typical of many memoirs by Holocaust survivors. Chapters are often short—bits, pieces, fragments—just as the full text may be short as well. This punctuated form of recounting serves two purposes at once. On one side, it allows memories to emerge; the pen's need "to go on and on" is satisfied to that degree. At the same moment, memory is kept in bounds. It does not go *too* far into the "deepness" from which one may not get out.

Retelling through discrete episodes or images thus characterized recounting within our conversations as it characterizes the form of this book. Reflections came as distinct moments. Gradually, their relationship with each other also emerged, along with their place in the trajectory of the whole. Chronology is a primary organizing frame, imposed here as it is imposed in most memoirs, following the less orderly way that memories usually first arise. At the same time, that frame also allows itself to be broken, as memories get ahead of themselves and, at times, behind. "One thought leads to the next, and into the past." That double trajectory is also recreated in *Reflections*.

Which one of us did the actual writing, putting pen to paper or fingers to keyboard? In the diary entries, of course, Agi did all of it. For the rest, we each did some, and read text aloud to each other, polishing and refining along the way. Because of our years of conversation, we typically had several potential versions of each reflection, many of which were transcribed and all of which we had revisited many times. Often, therefore, it was a question of deciding which version said it best—most concisely, clearly, or definitively—in the context of the emerging whole. Sometimes that meant returning to an earlier version; sometimes to a later one. Most often, the result was a composite that borrowed from a number of prior retellings.

Without question, my being both a psychologist and a playwright contributed significantly to our collaboration. Regarding the former, psychologists are certainly used to hearing the "same story" retold many times, in different contexts, and keeping track of its different iterations. We are also used to helping the process along—from the cliched "it sounds like you're saying" to all our other attempts to clarify intended meaning. Finally, we are used to the ways memory itself evolves and deepens, both in the contexts of an unfolding relationship and an unfolding life.

What was the danger of my own perspective unduly influencing Agi's? As described, finding the right word, the most elucidating word, was a fully collaborative process. Over the course of our conversations, if Agi was searching for a particular term, or it sounded to me like the one she first used might not convey all that she intended, I did not hesitate to suggest alternatives. In many instances, this kind of refining went back and forth several times—my suggestions evoking another word or phrasing from her, and, eventually, to a way of putting things that seemed to "nail it" for both of us. This is co-authorship in immediate practice, and by the time we completed a particular segment, we would be hard-pressed to say precisely how one thing led to the other. Once again, the retelling unfolded "between us," although the final decisions on text were always Agi's.

It is worth noting that a more prosaic kind of co-authorship is often part of telling the stories of our lives, not for the purposes of a written memoir, but simply as we share experiences. That is, we do not need a psychologist to reflect back what it "sounds like" we are saying or to help us make connections between various facets of our account. Our friends and colleagues do it all the time: "So it was kind of like this?" or "You mean it like that?" or "It was just like that other thing you were talking about." Casually as they are offered, if our friend's suggestions really clarify something, their analogy or connection may very well become part of our next retelling of "our story." Very rarely, however, will we recall how and from whom the latest version came.

Of course, there are risks in a co-authored memoir that go beyond the casual borrowing of everyday storytelling. Playwrights, like psychologists, also work hard to find the "right word," and, if they keep their focus on the priorities of the collaborative process, they can be useful interlocutors. The risk, of course, is that playwrights also like to create their own characters and cadences, particularly within stories that capture them. Further, I am a playwright who, by the end of these twenty-five years, had also been immersed in teaching and writing about the Holocaust. Much of that work itself reflected what I had learned from Agi. Still, it is not hard to imagine how my own assumptions could have gone beyond being "useful background."

The expectable temptations were there. Indeed, there were passages I imagined in the course of this project that do not appear in it. First, that is because, taken as I may have been by a particular phrasing or emphasis, I recognized that it was my way of putting it, not Agi's. Second, if my own ear let something get by, Agi's always seemed to catch it. Of course, neither one of us can be certain that we caught everything. But it certainly did happen that Agi would say about a suggestion of mine, "That's very nice. It sounds good. But it's you, not me." To the extent that one can ever be sure of such things, it seemed immediately apparent she was right.

Problems like this might have come up more often were it not for another facet of our collaboration, not easy to describe, but more essential than anything else. Above and beyond all the rest, we are an exceptionally good team. Different ages, different genders, entirely different life experiences—and yet, from the beginning, we somehow "understood each other." When we worked together over a particular problem in the writing—what to title something, where to begin a section, where to end it—it was quite common for us to hit upon the same solution simultaneously. We "mind readers," as Agi put it, anticipated each other all the time. "There we go again!" I can hear her exclaiming.

There is no formula for this, no training, no technique. It is simply two friends recognizing a chemistry that has no logic beyond the sheer fact that it exists, and how lucky they are that it does. It hardly needs to be said that this was also a psychological, even spiritual, kinship that went beyond issues of writing. In one of our early conversations, Agi exclaimed, "But who is interested in these reflections? This is for the inner soul, for the philosophers. But who is interested?" Of course, she knew that the person across the table from her was profoundly interested. But it still made sense to check in every now and then, and to hope that we were not alone.

Thus, tempted as I might have been to substitute my words

for Agi's, I also was not. Agi's voice is not the same as mine, but it has become a part of me. I hear it clearly when I think of her, and its rhythms are part of what I carry from all that we have shared. At the end of *Reflections*, Agi remembers her father's voice; specifically, the way he sang certain hymns in synagogue: "I remember how much joy he got out of singing that particular one. And when it comes up, he is again with me, and I am singing with him. It is the harmony of voices that makes the legacy, the way I tune myself to him."

I like to think that Agi's voice for me is something like the way she describes her father's voice for her. In the end, it is far more compelling to tune myself to her phrasing than to go off on my own. To say it differently, the song, as a human story, ultimately does not belong to either one of us. But it was vitally important to both of us that it be given voice. Because this is Agi's memoir, and this is Agi's life, we worked together all these years so that she could do so here.

—Henry Greenspan

Photo by Henry Greenspan

Agi, June 2006